GW00984617

MICHAEL JACKSON

Catherine Dineen

OMNIBUS PRESS
LONDON · NEW YORK · SYDNEY

Edited by Chris Charleworth
Cover & Book designed by 4i Limited
Picture research by David Brolan

ISBN: 0.7119.3216.6
Order No: OP 47188

Exclusive distributors:

Book Sales Limited,
8/9 Frith Street,
London W1V 5TZ, UK.

Music Sales Corporation,
225 Park Avenue South,
New York, NY 10003, USA.

Music Sales Pty Ltd,
120 Rothschild Avenue,
Rosebery, NSW 2018, Australia.

To the Music Trade only:

Music Sales Limited,
8/9 Frith Street,
London W1V 5TZ, UK.

Photo credits:

All Action (front cover); ; Mark Anderson/Retna: 76b; Fin
Costello/Redferns: 14, 45; Famous: back cover (right), 19, 25,
31, 34, 38, 65, 83, 91, 95, 96t; Gary Gershoff/Retna: 81; Steve
Granitz/Retna: 92; Robin Kaplan/Retna: 62; Phil Loftus/Retna: 33,
96b; London Features International: 6, 7, 10, 13, 15, 16, 18, 20,
21, 22, 23, 24, 26, 27 28, 32, 36, 37, 39, 41, 43, 44, 47, 48, 50,
51, 52, 53b, 54, 56, 57, 58, 60, 66, 67, 70, 72, 74, 75, 80, 82, 84,
87, 89, 94; Pictorial Press: 9, 12, 40b, 59, 78, 85; Barry Plummer:
8, 11, 17, 46, 55, 53t; Michael Putland/Retna: 5; Retna: 35; Steve
Rapport/Retna: back cover (left); Rex Features: 29, 30, 69, 76t,
90, 93; Chase Roe/Retna: 63; Laurie Stoll/Retna: 40t.

Printed and bound in Great Britain by Scotprint Limited,
Musselburgh, Scotland.

A catalogue record for this book is available from the
British Library.

CONTENTS

INTRODUCTION

No pop artist in the last ten years has been heard more widely than Michael Jackson. The 1982 album 'Thriller' and its excellent predecessor 'Off The Wall' established him as a mature maestro able to blend contemporary styles - pop, soul, rock - into a blockbusting commercial sound. And when he eventually took the music on the road, the stage show was a breathtaking mixture of extraordinary dancing full of athleticism, grace and imagination with a strong visual and theatrical sensibility.

But Jackson the unparalleled pop phenomenon remained a hazy, enigmatic human being who obsessively shunned the limelight as assiduously as he courted it on stage. There were sound reasons for this, as you'll read, not the least of which were death threats.

Michael Joe Jackson was born in Gary, Indiana, on August 29, 1956, the seventh of nine children. He was a natural performer and once he grabbed centre-stage during rehearsals with his brothers' group at the age of four he never let it go. With Berry Gordy's Tamla Motown organisation, The Jackson 5 reeled off four straight number one hits, starting with 'I Want You Back' in 1970.

During these early years Michael talks much like any other kid - inquisitive, funny, a bit naïve - and there is also clear evidence of quotes learned carefully at the behest of Motown, particularly about the group's "discovery" by Diana Ross, which was merely a publicity stunt.

By the time the Jackson 5 left Motown in the mid-Sixties, forcing a split with brother Jermaine, Michael became his own man, definite about direction and what he wanted to attain. Towards the end of the decade, as his work became more confident and assured, most noticeably after he worked on the film *The Wiz*, in which he provided the only genuinely memorable moments, and with Quincy Jones on 1979's 'Off The Wall', Jackson himself became less outgoing.

In his late teens he'd grown tall quickly and suffered from acne and, as his sister LaToya insists in her autobiography, Michael and all of his brothers and sisters were subjected to considerable mental pressure and physical intimidation by their father, Joseph. He also mocked Michael's appearance, which encouraged the young man to take steps to alter his nose and chin.

The more famous he became, the less accessible he was, but he is certainly not alone in this. After 'Thriller' with its 40 million-plus sales, his every move was open to public scrutiny which made him even more retiring and defensive. His menagerie of pets, love of Disneyland and cartoons, affinity with children, friendships with much older film stars and generally quirky behaviour and odd desires made him excellent tabloid fodder. Yet his closest friends find sound reasons and understanding for most of these supposed excesses. And co-existing in the same head as this unusual personality is a businessman with a sharp mind able to make hard decisions.

Michael Jackson is a conundrum. But through careful reading of his own words, and those of his family, friends and working colleagues, who he is, the man he is, becomes less of a puzzle.

Catherine Dineen, October 1992.

EARLY DAYS

I would like to be a great entertainer... I want peace for the world and I'd like to own my own mansion one day. **Michael, at 5, listing three wishes in kindergarten.**

We started singing together after Tito started messin' with Dad's guitar and singing with the radio. It was Tito [who] decided we should form a group and we did and we practised a lot and then we started entering talent shows and we won every one we entered.

Those talent shows were our professional education.

We used to rehearse all the time in Gary. Every day when we came home from school... My father used to make us keep going and he put it in our heads that practice makes perfect. Now I understand what he was trying to do.

The thing I remember most from those days - and the reason we are here today as entertainers - was rehearsing for seven hours every day. Straight after school, perfecting ourselves and with our father teaching us. Though he had a group, he was never a real showman but he knew exactly what I had to do to become a professional. He taught me exactly how to hold a mike and make gestures to the crowd and how to handle an audience... he was the best teacher we could have had.

[Michael remembers] A huge baseball pitch at the back of where we lived and children playing and eating popcorn and everything... I didn't really feel left out. We got a lot in exchange for not playing baseball in the summer. My father was always very protective of us, taking care of business and everything.

[His father] can be very hard... sometimes. You don't wanna be gettin' him mad. He's strict, but we never object. That's how he wants it, so we go along. He shows us the value of work and hard effort.

It's not hard. You just have to put your mind to what you're doin', that's all there is to it. **Michael's secret revealed in 1971.**

I think that to start early is the best way in any field of endeavour. I just thank God for the talent.

THE JACKSON 5 IN THE EARLY DAYS. BACK ROW, FROM LEFT: JERMAINE, MICHAEL AND JACKIE; FRONT: MARLON AND TITO.

MICHAEL AND MARLON.

To tell you the truth, it just came out naturally and I'd just sing and it came out sounding nice to me.

I'm still amazed at how my voice used to sound. They used to tell me that I had the voice of a 35-year-old when it comes to phrasing and control. I have been singing since I was five years old, so by the time I began to make those first records, I'd already had five or six years' experience.

I'll tell you the honest-to-God truth. I never knew what I was doing in the early days - I just did it. I never knew how I sang, I didn't really control it, it just formed itself.

I used to come home from school at three and everything would be set up in the living room, the drums and all, and we practised until night and we kept on and kept on and had different meetings and stuff and we used to wonder, "When will we have a show?"

[The first gig] was in a shopping centre, The Big Top, in Gary, Indiana. It was a grand opening. All the people come round to buy the season fashions. We agreed to be in front of the mall, in the middle of it, and sing. I was about six. I got started around five.

We did a couple of things for schools and they were in the paper and a couple of days later we did a talent show for the mayor [Richard Hatcher] and he invited his guest, Diana Ross, who was visiting Gary, Indiana, and was a good friend of his, to see it. She liked us and she came backstage and told us that she liked the act and she took us to Motown where we auditioned with a couple of numbers and they liked the act too.

Then we did this benefit for the mayor [Richard Hatcher of Gary, Indiana] and Diana Ross was in the audience, and afterwards we was in the dressing room and Diana Ross knocked on the door and she brought us to Motown in Detroit and that was it. **Two versions of Michael's well-rehearsed story of how Tamla Motown discovered the Jackson 5. Much of it was false.**

One day Gladys Knight told a guy named Bobby Taylor [of The Vancouvers] at Motown about us, and Motown got a hold of us. We did a show on Berry [Gordy's] gigantic estate in Detroit, around the poolside. **A more accurate version of how they got to Motown.**

When we auditioned for Berry [Gordy] in Detroit, Diana came over and she kissed us and said that we were going to go a long, long way and that she wanted to be a part of it - and that's what she did. In the things we have done together - such as *The Wiz* or the TV specials - she has been for us 100% and making sure that everything was done for us that could be done.

I had just about given up hope. I thought I was going to be an old man before being discovered, but along came Miss Diana Ross to save my career. **At the party to introduce the Jackson Five.**

We were doing a theatre in Chicago called the Regal, which was kind of an audition for Motown. Since Diana Ross was the hottest artist there at the time, they decided to use her name to introduce us to the public.

THE JACKSON 5 WITH DIANA ROSS.

JAMES BROWN.

I liked being on the Diana Ross special. It wasn't hard learning the lines 'cos they had cards with the lines written out. *Later, he would be less free with showbiz secrets.*

Diana was - and still is - like an overseer for the whole group. As well as Berry Gordy, they were the two. Berry has only ever managed two groups in the whole Motown history - The Supremes and the Jackson 5.

We were working fewer hours than we wanted to because of the Child Labour Act.

We used to do these club shows, and there was this one lady - you probably know what she did - but I thought it was awful. I was around six, and she was one of those stripteasers, and she would take her drawers off, and a man would come up, and they'd start doing - aw man, she was too funky. Ugh! That, to me, was awful!

My pockets would be loaded with money. Because people would throw money on the stage. We would have around $300 lying on the stage, and we would make just $15 from the manager paying us.

Boy loved his waffles is all I know. Loved my waffles. Got my Michael safe in my head. Don't know who-all that boy is in the sparkly soldier suits. **Anna Wilson, Jackson 5 landlady in New York during their first Apollo gigs.**

[James Brown] is so magic. I'd be in the wings when I was, like, six or seven. I'd sit there and watch him. He's the most electrifying. He can take an audience anywhere he wants to. The audience just went bananas. He went wild... he gets so out of himself. **Michael, 24, recalling a major influence.**

I had to work to get him away from a lot of it. **Suzanne de Passe, Motown employee who coached the Jackson 5 stage show.**

When James Brown or Sammy Davis, Jr came on it was exciting to me - and they still are my idols today.

[James Brown] don't get the credit he should get from the music industry. Look what he did to music: all these funky tracks that you hear today, that's where it came from. Sly Stone, James Brown, these are people that started funky music. They stood between the gospelly soul and the dance music. And that's funk: Sly, James Brown, and people like Wilson Pickett, Otis Redding. And of course in rock and roll there's Little Richard and Chuck Berry and all those guys. That's who I would watch. And Jackie Wilson - yeow!

I like to start with the origin of things, because once it gets along it changes. It's so interesting to see how it really was in the beginning. **On listening to James Brown, Ray Charles, Jackie Wilson, Chuck Berry, Little Richard.**

My dancing just comes about spontaneously. Some things I've done for years until people have marked them as my style, but it's all spontaneous reactions. People have named certain dances after me, like the spin I do, but I can't even remember how I started the spin - it just came about.

OUTSIDE HAMMERSMITH ODEON, LONDON, IN 1977.

[Motown] took care to develop each individual person. Like, Tito likes cars and mechanics, and Jackie likes basketball and I draw cartoons. With a lot of groups, you know the group's name but you don't know each individual. That was very important to us.

I was on a living geography lesson, you can't get much better than that.

I like classical music and soft listening music. Sometimes I sit and listen to soft stuff like Johnny Mathis. I like Ray Charles. And most of the time, I listen to Three Dog Night. **Well, he was only 11!**

Tito always ended up wetting the bed. We'd always have a yellow mattress... hey, Yellow Mattress! That's a good name for an album title. **On the joys of room-sharing with his brothers.**

It was hard. Money was short. It was a drag.

[My sisters] never wanted to be in the group. Besides, if we let Janet in the group she'd have eaten up all the profits.

I'm kind of excited [about the 1972 tour of England]. I want to see some sights. Which place is Napoleon in? *[In France, dead.]* Oh, right. I would like to go there too. In London I'd like to go to the stores and get some clothes. **The 13-year-old tourist.**

I'm good on my trampoline and I'm good at pool. **The 12-year-old hustler.**

Girls chase me. That's why we need our security.

If it weren't for the screaming, it wouldn't be exciting. The kids help us being the way they are.

We have security guards that line the stage. If they weren't there I'd be nervous. At most of our concerts, girls try to get past the police and if the guards weren't there, I would be expecting something bad to happen. But I'm not afraid. All they ever want to do is touch you or get your autograph. They don't want to do anything to hurt you. **This was his view in 1972. Much later, he was less sure about the last part.**

We used to live in a small house, now we have a big one with a studio and a music room plus some of the things we always wanted. Like we always wanted a basketball court. In Gary, we would walk a couple of miles to a basketball court but now we just all go out there and play.

We moved because the houses were too close. We built a studio in the house - sixteen track - and when we'd rehearse the neighbours would complain. So we moved. Only one star complained. Frank Sinatra lived right above us. No, he never complained. But his balcony was right over us.

I used to go to places by myself, far away places, not just the store. There's a big difference now. I can go to the store now by myself but when we go to far away places, like the movies, go-kart racing, horseback riding, we have to take security with us. If we go without security, they tell us that we should have because kids will recognise us. People know we live in LA. Sometimes the mailman gets a letter addressed 'Jackson 5' with no address and he knows where to bring it. **The 13-year-old slowly realising what celebrity means.**

I like what I'm doing. I do have a lot of friends outside show business too and they treat us regular.

Hi! I'm Michael! I used to be 12 and cute. Now I'm 16 and cute. **His nightly introduction at the Jackson 5 Las Vegas shows.**

We keep [our stage uniforms]. We have three rooms packed full of them. We have all our old stuff way back to the Ed Sullivan Show.

We have fun, we really do. I guess I can understand what it is that bugs [teenybop star] David Cassidy but I've sure got no complaints. As far as I'm concerned everything's fine. I certainly don't want to quit. **Michael was 15 when asked if he wanted to retire.**

We got to meet the Queen [in 1976, at a Royal Command Performance] and she seemed to

be genuinely interested in us and asked where we came from and how we got started. The Duke [of Edinburgh] asked us whether our family was in show business before us and whether we played instruments. It was really nice.

What are truffles? I like meat and potatoes. I drink a lot of water. Is that caviar? I'm not too anxious to [try some]. Maybe just a little. Do you honestly like this stuff? I can't understand that. How could anybody eat this stuff? **Michael, 18, at lunch with Andy Warhol and friends.**

I've never been on a date - outside of *The Dating Game.* And that was work. **Michael, 18.**

When we first lost our original name, we felt lost. You see, we had the name long before we thought of signing with Motown and it was our identity. But, as time has gone on, it seems to matter less and less and today we are identified as The Jacksons just as readily, so it hasn't done any permanent damage. People still think of us as the Jackson 5, anyway.

RANDY, ON MICHAEL'S SHOULDER, JOINS THE BAND.

SONGS, WRITING & LPs

MICHAEL FRONTS THE JACKSONS DURING THE TAMLA MOTOWN 25TH ANNIVERSARY SPECIAL.

2

WITH THE JACKSON 5 AND THE JACKSONS

There's no use creating music that people don't want. The object is to bring joy into other people's lives.

Certain people were created for certain things, and I think our job is to entertain the world. I don't see no other thing that I could be doing.

People seem to think that because The Osmonds became big with records that sounded something like ours we should have something against them. But it's not like that. I think they're a good group and I certainly have nothing against them.

I feel [imitation by other acts] is a compliment in one way, and in another way you be kinda angry. Because it's yours. We were the first young group out there with that style, making hit records. There were nobody out there at our age. We came across it, and then all of a sudden along came The Osmonds, The Partridge Family. Now you have groups like The Sylvers. The Sylvers have the same producer that wrote all our hits, Freddie Perren. That's why they sound so much like us.

I can forget all kinds of things, but I'll never forget a melody.

Motown producers didn't let you sing freely, they told you what to sing. When we started that was fine. But later on...

All those [Motown] records in the past are our songs, and we've sung them, and we put our hearts into the singing of them, but they're really not from us. They're not our thoughts and what we think should go on that plastic, on that wax.

I mainly like ['Ben'] as a record. I love rats. And I like it as a friend, too, as if I'm talking to a guy that's a friend of mine - but none other than just a friend! Some people see it the rat way. Some people see it the friend way. It works both ways.

I just hate everyday love songs. I'm interested in a different type of love song. I want a brand-new thought. That's what I love about 'Ben'. There's a mystery to it... so many people come up to me and say, "Why did you create such a song about a little stinkin' rat? How'd you make it so beautiful if it's about a dumb rat?"

It's so much easier to write that way [as a group]. Everybody has a different point of view and something different to add. **On The Jacksons' 10th anniversary.**

I like it, and if I like it, I know [the public] will. I keep up with the songs and the times. I feel we know what's happening.

I spend a lot of time with my songs. I want to make them perfect, really good. Each time I write a song, I think to myself that this has to be a Top Ten record. I have more trouble with the lyrics than the music, so I write a lot with Jermaine. All you need for a hit record is the right kind of feeling.

I write about all kinda things. I write about an old man, a tree, what's happening in the world, a deer. I love writing so much I'd eat it, really. I love it.

I want to get into other things. I just cut some tracks with Glen Campbell.

'Destiny' [The Jacksons' 1978 album] was the beginning of the whole thing and the timing was so right. But there is so much still to come and for ['Triumph'] we are so much open and freer. We are all really excited about it.

['Destiny'] broke the ice for us as producers, too. The song is actually about me and has a deep, deep meaning for us. But it also provided a direction for the future and we are thinking of calling the next album 'Foundation'. *[It became 'Triumph'.]*

I was trying to step into the future with ['Heartbreak Hotel'], trying something different, integrating drama and sound effects with music. And it worked. **The track, which Michael wrote for The Jacksons' 'Triumph' (1980), is the first example of what would become his solo style.**

SOLO

I could never go solo, not with the group being a family thing because it would be like breaking away from my family. Anyway, the other guys are doing some solo things too and we're still recording as a group.

Motown decided to take a chance on me with the solo albums. It's up to the public, it's like a vote, they decide to pick you. We've travelled the world, and if we don't sing 'Ben' they all go crazy. I could never believe how big that song was. I haven't done a solo album in a long time but I will be doing some more.

Those were good songs, I like those songs a lot. But especially, I like the new songs. **Introducing 'Billie Jean' at the Motown 25th anniversary concerts having sung Jackson 5 and The Jacksons' songs**

One day, I called Quincy [Jones] up to ask if he could suggest some great people who might want to do my album ['Off The Wall']. It was the first time that I fully wrote and produced my songs and I was looking for somebody who would give me that freedom plus somebody who's unlimited musically.

QUINCY JONES.

Quincy calls me Smelly and he said, "Well Smelly, why don't you let me do it?" I said "That's a great idea." I sounded so phoney, like I was trying to hint to that - but I wasn't. I didn't even think of that. But Quincy does jazz, movie scores, rock'n'roll, funk, pop - he's all colours and that's the kind of people I like to work with. I went over to his house just about every other day and we just put it together.

Working with Quincy, I learned so much and I'm greedy for knowledge. For me, to learn something I've always hungered for makes me happy. I'll never forget watching him work because he knows no limitations.

When Quincy and I first started ['Off The Wall'] we sat down and discussed exactly what

we wanted and it has all turned out the way we planned. We pre-decided the whole make-up of the album but, if anything, it has done more than we expected. We aimed for triple platinum and now it's on its way to five million!

'Working Day And Night' is very autobiographical in a lot of ways, though I did stretch a point to playing the part like I was married to this person and she's got me moving.

The next [album after 'Off the Wall'] has to be three times as great... it can't be just as good because that would be a letdown. So I'll just take my time and get it right.

[Quincy] made me drive all the way to my

ON STAGE DURING THE VICTORY TOUR.

house, and he forced me to get the engineer in to do this song... and I made him wait in the other room. I was really embarrassed. I was in there, singing my heart out. So finally, I was done. He came in, and I played it. And when it was over, he just loved it! He hugged me and said "This is the song we've been looking for". **On 'Beat It'.**

I wanted to write a song, the type of song that I would buy if I wanted a rock song. That is how I approached it and I wanted the kids to enjoy it. The next thing I can recall is the song being there. I think the gift is there naturally but the songs come through me. **On 'Beat It'.**

When composing the song 'Heal The World' it was my dream to hear it performed the way they [a boys' choir] just performed it... It took everything to keep me from crying.

I wrote 'Will You Be There?' [off 'Dangerous'] at my house, Never Never Land in California. I didn't think about it hard. I always feel that it's done from above. I feel fortunate for being that instrument through which music flows. I'm just the source through which it comes. I can't take credit for it because it's God's work. He's just using me as the messenger.

I wake up from dreams and go "Wow, put this down on paper." The whole thing is strange. You hear the words, everything is right there in front of your face... That's why I hate to take credit for the songs I've written. I feel that somewhere, someplace, it's been done and I'm just a courier bringing it out into the world.

I really believe that God chooses people to do certain things, the way Michelangelo or Leonardo da Vinci or Mozart or Muhammed Ali or Martin Luther King is chosen... I haven't scratched the surface yet of what my real purpose is for being here. I'm committed to my art. I believe that all art has as its ultimate goal that union between the material and the spiritual, the human and the divine.

That's what I'm here for really. It's like Michelangelo or Leonardo da Vinci. Today we can still see their work and be inspired by it. I'd like to just keep going and inspire people and try new things.

I feel that this world we live in is really a big, huge, monumental symphonic orchestra. I believe that in its primordial form, all of creation is sound and that it's not just random sound, that it's music. You've heard the expression "the music of the spheres"? Well, that's a very literal phrase.

The same music governs the rhythm of the seasons, the pulse of our heartbeats, the migration of the birds, the ebb and flow of ocean tides, the cycles of growth, evolution and dissolution. It's music, it's rhythm.

No matter what you do you are competing against your previous product and everybody expects more. Just like motion pictures. *Raiders Of The Lost Ark, Star Wars, Jedi.* You really try to top yourself all the time and it's hard - like The Bee Gees and 'Saturday Night Fever'. But I believe in doing better work. Just like the old saying, "You don't get older, you get better."

I wanted to do an album that was like Tchaikovsky's 'Nutcracker Suite' so that in a thousand years from now, people would still be listening to it. Something that would live forever. I would like to see children and teenagers and parents and all races all over the world, hundreds and hundreds of years from now, still pulling out songs from that album and dissecting it. I want it to live. **On 'Dangerous'.**

My goal in life is to give to the world what I was lucky to receive: the ecstasy of divine union through my music and dance.

PRODUCING

Well, I've done a single called 'Night Time Lover' on my sister LaToya's album, that will be released on Polydor real soon. **[In her autobiography, LaToya accuses Michael of sabotaging the track through jealousy.]**

I co-produced 'Don't Stop ['Til You Get Enough]' with Quincy, and I also arranged that one. And my brother Randy and I co-produced 'Shake Your Body [Down To The Ground]'.

ON STAGE DURING THE BAD TOUR.

SHOWTIME ! !

3

We're so silly when we're on the road and we just get sillier. We play games, we throw things at each other. It seems like when you're under pressure you find some kind of escapism to make up for that because the road is a lot of tensions: work, interviews, fans grabbing at you, everybody wants a piece of you, you're always busy, the phone's ringing all night with fans calling you, so you put the phone under the mattress, then the fans knock at the door screaming, you can't even get out of the room without them following you. You feel that all around you. It's like you're in a goldfish bowl and they're watching you.

I wouldn't say I was sexy. But I guess that's fine if that's what they say... I just do it really. The sex thing is kind of spontaneous. It really creates itself, I think.

Once the music plays, it creates me. The instruments move me, through me, they control me.

When I look at the audience and see people of different races holding hands and rocking together it makes me feel great.

In a crowd, I'm afraid. On stage, I'm safe. I'd sleep on stage if I could. See, my whole life has been on stage and the impression I get of people is applause, standing ovations and running after you.

I was raised on stage and I am more comfortable out there than I am right now [being interviewed]. When it comes time to get off, I don't want to. I feel like there are angels protecting me. I could sleep on stage.

Do you like doing [interviews]? I really do hate this. I am much more relaxed on stage than I am right now.

I just love what I'm doing and I believe in training and getting better. It's like a church type of thing when the spirit gets inside somebody and they lose self control. I'm a totally different person when I'm dancing.

Sometimes you get to a note and that note will touch the whole audience. What they're throwing out at you, you're grabbing. You hold it, you touch it, and you whip it back - it's like a Frisbee.

I can't perform if I don't have that kind of ping-pong with the crowd. You know, the kind of cause and effect action, reaction. Because I play off them. They're really feeding me and I'm just acting from their energy.

I sit there [at other artists' concerts] and say, "Please don't call me up, I am too shy". But once I get up there, I take control of myself. Being on stage is magic. There's nothing like it. You feel the energy of everybody who's out there. You feel it all over your body. When the lights hit you, it's all over, I swear it is.

When it's time to go off, I don't want to. I could stay up there for ever. It's the same thing with making a movie. What's wonderful about a film is that you can become another person. I love to forget. And lots of times, you totally forget. It's like automatic pilot.

Pilots tell me, "I wish there were no such thing as having to go down and re-load with fuel. I wish I could stay up here forever. For ever. This is the safest place in the world for me". And I totally understand what they mean. When I'm into 40,000 people, it's so easy. Nothing can harm me when I'm on stage - nothing. That's really me. That's what I'm here to do. I'm totally at home on stage. That's where I live. That's where I was born. That's where I'm safe.

I love what I do. I'm happy at what I do. It's escapism.

I love being on stage and I enjoy seeing different cities and experiencing cultures, environments and the local arts and languages.

When Jermaine left I used to feel a bit naked on stage because I was so used to turning to him and seeing him on my left.

The other day I got a letter from a girl in Texas named Ladonnia Jones. She'd been saving her money from odd jobs to buy a ticket, but with the current tour system she'd have to buy four tickets and she couldn't afford that. So I've asked our promoter to work out a new way of distributing tickets - a way that no longer requires a $120 money order... I've asked our promoter to end the mail order system as soon as possible so that no one will pay money unless they get a ticket. **[A prepared statement on the eve of the Victory tour first night following the furore over inflated ticket prices and punitive and unwieldy application procedures.]**

When I first agreed to [do the Victory] tour I decided to donate all the money I make from our performances to charity.

It's been a long twenty years. This is our final farewell tour as a family. **At the end of the group's 1984 Victory tour.**

For different people, growing up can occur at a different age and now I'm showing the world that I'm the man I always wanted to be. **On the Bad tour.**

The only reason I am going on [the Dangerous tour] is to raise funds for the newly-formed Heal The World Foundation, an international children's charity, that I am spearheading to assist children and the ecology. My goal is to gross $100m by Christmas 1993. I urge every corporation and individual who cares about this planet and the future of the children to help raise money for the charity.

The Heal The World Foundation will contribute funds to paediatric aids in honour of my friend, Ryan White. I am looking forward to this tour because it will allow me to devote time to visiting children all around the world, as well as spread the message of global love, in the hope that others will be moved to do their share to help heal the world.

Michael's vision is to present the most spectacular, most state-of-the-art show to the world that it has ever seen, and that's the goal we're moving toward. **Benny Collins, production executive on the Dangerous tour.**

MICHAEL AND HIS WAXWORK FIGURE
AT MADAME TUSSAUD'S IN LONDON.

FANS & FRIENDS, PEOPLE & PLACES

I hate it when I meet fans and they try and tear bits of my hair and clothing. It's like they're trying to tear your soul away. I feel like spaghetti being pulled every which way.

You don't get peace in a shop. If they don't know your name, they know your voice. And you can't hide. Being mobbed hurts. You feel like you're spaghetti among thousands of hands. They're just ripping and pulling your hair. And you feel that any moment you're gonna just break.

I still get so many letters asking if I had a sex change or if I go with guys or thinking I'm married to Clifton Davis.

Girls in the lobby, coming up the stairway. You hear guards getting them out of elevators. But you stay in your room and write a song. And when you get tired of that, you talk to yourself. Then let it all out on-stage. That's what it's like.

I love meeting the fans because that's why we go on tour - to come face to face with the people who buy the records. You never get the chance to actually see them put the needle on the record so being on tour is the closest you can get. [It's] wonderful to know that the people in the audience enjoy your music and have your albums at home.

A lot of people can't deal with the fact that you're another person on stage. They'll come up to me and say, "Sing us a couple of bars of 'Rock With You'" or "Do that spin that you do on TV". And I'm really embarrassed. If two people come up to me on the street, then it's hard.

There are times when I wish I could be just like everybody else. For example, there are only two places that I can go shopping - New York and London. And sometimes they'll close down the whole store just so that I can shop there. Diana [Ross] does it all the time. They'll close down a whole Mall for her!

There are times when I wish I weren't so recognisable and I could just go out and have a good time. Like being able to go to Disneyland and just go on the rides.

[Jesus] preached and people came about Him. He didn't get angry and push them aside and say "Leave Me alone". I'm not calling myself Jesus but I'm comparing the stress and pressure to Jesus.

I love the fans and they are the reason for my professional existence. When I'm out there

4

doing a show and I see the fans dancing and singing, that's what I love the most. It's just the greatest feeling in the world.

It is the worst thing in the world for me to let my fans down. Thank you for all of your patience and grace yesterday. **After cancelling a concert at Wembley Arena on August 1, 1992.**

THE FANS SAY...

Dear Michael, I have a problem. I've been in LOVE with you ever since I set my eyes on you. I would like to see you in person. My birthday is March 3 and I will be 11. I hope I am not too old for you. **Fan Carla Hall in a letter to** *Soul* **magazine, 1970.**

There have been more camera crews than people. [Michael's] been in here a few times. He won't look you straight in the eye. He's a shy guy, I guess, but he will sign autographs which is more than Prince does... Michael used to sign with whatever date it was. Now he signs 1998. I don't know what that means. Maybe it's when he thinks the world is going to end. **Todd Meehan, Tower Records, Los Angeles.**

It was worth it. He was fabulous on the phone. I talked for quite a while with him. He sounded a very warm person. He told me not to do it again - to stay together. Of course, I am going to. He basically saved my life. If he hadn't come out, I obviously would have jumped. **Eric Herminie, who had threatened to jump off the roof of a building opposite the Dorchester Hotel, where Michael stayed in 1992.**

THE SUPREMES IN 1965, LEFT TO RIGHT: FLORENCE BALLARD, MARY WILSON AND DIANA ROSS.

FRIENDS

If I'm seen around with lots of different [girls] I'm made out to be some kind of sex maniac. If I go out with anyone for any length of time everybody tries to marry me off.

Diana Ross

She always tells me her most private secrets. That's the kind of relationship we have.

She's a real, real, mother. We met her when we auditioned for Berry Gordy at his mansion in Detroit... we auditioned at the poolside. All the Motown stars were there and Diana came over and told us how much she loved us and wanted to play a big part in our career. So she introduced us to the public. Our first hit album was called 'Diana Ross Presents The Jackson 5'.

Liza Minelli

When I was filming *The Wiz* in New York, I danced almost every night at Studio 54 with Liza Minelli. We'd talk about Judy Garland.

The only time I've danced somewhere like [Studio 54] is when Liza Minelli will come in and she'll just pull me on the floor. She's so aggressive.

DIANA ROSS IN THE MID-SEVENTIES.

She's like me, an old showbiz kid. I just love her to death. When we get together, it's all show talk. I show her my favourite pair of gold lamé underpants and she shows me her favourite dance steps.

Me and Liza, say. Now I would consider her a great friend but a show business friend. And we're sitting there talking about this movie and she'll tell me about Judy Garland. And then she'll go, "Show me that stuff you did at rehearsal". And I'll go, "Show me yours". We're totally into each other's performance.

Brooke Shields

I love people like Brooke, who are talented but who work so hard. Brooke is a nice girl but she's not Elizabeth Taylor. That's the kind of lady I want to be seen with.

MICHAEL WITH ELIZABETH TAYLOR.

Katharine Hepburn

There's a lot of people Katharine doesn't like. I feel honoured to be counted among her friends.

Jane Fonda

We talk about all kinds of things. Politics, philosophers, racism, Vietnam and acting. It's magic.

She wants to do so many projects with me. She saw The Wiz about six times and she said there's so much more for me to do. I feel the same way.

To Andy Warhol

You know who I always see you with? I don't know why but when I usually see a picture of you, you're usually with Alfred Hitchcock. I thought you were brothers or something. Did you interview him? He talks funny, doesn't he?

Paul McCartney

The first time I met Paul McCartney was on the Queen Mary, and then I met him again at a party he threw at Harold Lloyd's estate here in LA. Him and Linda came up to me and said, "We wrote you a song" and they started singing 'Girlfriend'. I said, "I really like it, when can we get together?" So he gave me his Scotland number and the number in London... The next time I noticed it, he had the song on his 'London Town' album. Then one day I went to Quincy's house and he said, "You know what's a great song for you? This McCartney song 'Girlfriend'." I just flipped out.

Paul McCartney sent me a telegram not too long ago raving over how much he loved mine better than his and now I'm going to be doing some things on his next album.

I'm a collector of cartoons. All the Disney stuff, Bugs Bunny, the old MGM ones. I've only met one person who has a bigger collection than I do and I was surprised - Paul McCartney. He's a cartoon

fanatic. Whenever I go to his house, we watch cartoons. When we came here to work on my album ['Off The Wall'], we rented all these cartoons from the studio. Dumbo and some other stuff. It's real escapism. It's like "Everything's all right". It's like the world is in a faraway city. Everything's fine.

Fred Astaire

He's a friend of mine and he's said some wonderful compliments. We didn't live too far from him in Beverly Hills and he tells me he used to see me every day riding around on my motor bike and he'd blow his horn. He told me he loves my work and I'm doing a lot of things that he wasn't even doing when he first started.

He told me him and Ginger Rogers would do a whole dance number for three months. Who practises like that today? Nobody. And they should. You can tell perfection by looking at it.

Julie Andrews

When she shook my hand she shook it real hard. She said, "My daughter Emma has your album and we love what you're doing so much". And I said, "You don't know what you've done for me by your work." She's been so influential. You know the front of *The Sound Of Music* when Julie Andrews runs up on that mountain and she throws her arms out? Oh! I can eat that... that's the whole wonder of motion pictures.

PETS, KIDS AND PLACES

I'm crazy for kids and animals and puppies. And I love exotic things. I've had llamas, peacocks, a rhea, a macaw, pheasants, raccoons, chickens... now I'm gonna get a fawn. And a flamingo. I don't think I want a cougar but I want a chimpanzee - they're so sweet. Oooooh, I have such a good time with the animals.

I have two fawns. Mr Tibbs looks like a ram, he's got the horns. I've got a beautiful llama. His name is Louie. This is Muscles [boa constrictor] and I have trained him to eat interviewers. Snakes are very misunderstood. Bad press.

When I got my llamas I would make this certain crazy vocabulary and they would understand and come running.

The whole godly instinct thing is just so incredible. I can never get over it.

I guess I want to bring [his manikins] to life. I like to imagine talking to them. You know what I think it is? I think I'm accompanying myself with friends I never had. I probably have two friends.

MICHAEL VISITS QUEEN ELIZABETH'S CHILDREN'S HOSPITAL IN HACKNEY, 1992.

Being an entertainer, you just can't tell who is your friend. They see you so differently, a star instead of a next door neighbour. I surround myself with people I want to be my friends. And I can do that with manikins. I'll talk to them.

There's a certain sense that animals and children have that gives me a certain creative juice, a certain force that later on in adulthood is kind of lost because of the conditioning that happens in the world.

They are the way I wish the world really was because they are not phoney and they don't know prejudice. Prejudice is taught. If the world were full of only children it would be a much better place.

One of my favourite pastimes is being with children - talking to them, playing with them... they're one of the main reasons why I do what I do. [They] know everything that people are trying to find out but it's hard for them to get it out. I can recognise that and learn from it. They go through brilliant, genius stages but when they become a certain age, they lose it.

Children are the most brilliant people of all, that's why they relate to those stories [*Wizard of Oz, Peter Pan*] so well. Fairy tales are wonderful. What more can you ask for, outside of conquering goals and believing in your ideas.

The innocence of children represents to me the source of infinite creativity. That is the potential of every human being. But by the time you're an adult, you're conditioned.

Grown-ups are really nothing but children who have lost all that real magic by not noticing and digging and finding out.

Michael: Do you have any kids?
Andy Warhol: Me? I don't believe in marrying.
MJ: Really? Why not?
AW: I don't believe in love.
MJ: Really? You don't? You just date?
AW: Yes, I like to date.
MJ: Do you live alone?
AW: With my dogs.

I heard on the news that this little boy had his Christmas a month ahead of time, and Santa Claus at his house, because he only had a week to live. Sure enough, in that week he died - and that just made me so sad. I meet children like that all the time when we visit the hospitals... They say "You've got to meet this girl, she's going to die tomorrow and ever since she's been out of surgery she's been calling your name". And, God, I just feel so wonderful to be part of somebody's ultimate dream. All my lifetime of work is rewarded.

I'll tell [fatally ill] kids, "I'll see you next year" and

sometimes the thought that I'll be back next year makes them hang on. That's happened several times.

Our children are the most beautiful, most sweet, most treasured of our creations. And yet, every minute at least 28 children die. Today our children are at risk of being killed by disease, and by the violence of war, guns, abuse, and neglect. Children have few rights and no one to speak for them. They have no voice in the world. Please, join with me and the children to help heal the world. Together, parents, communities, governments - all people of the world - we must put our children first.

I love Switzerland. It's so clean and cool. We don't get much snow where I live, so I get real excited in Lausanne or Geneva. I'd like to buy a house there when I'm older and settle down. It's all so cute that it looks like a movie set.

I love Miami and I love the nature of Switzerland. It takes your breath away - the mountains and the valleys are so beautiful, it's like a storybook country and every place is like a postcard picture. I promised myself that I would one day own a house in Switzerland and it's a promise I'll keep to myself.

Holland is the Europe that you dream about. London, England's city, can look like New York - a little - but if you go to Holland, man, you know it's real Europe. And Scotland is - I could eat it, it's so beautiful. You know it's not America.

I get a taste of poverty too. When I go to a country - like in the Philippines and Trinidad and in Africa - I really get out and go to the poor sections and talk to the people. I sit in their little huts, their cardboard houses and I make myself at home. I think it's important to know how different people feel, especially in my field of endeavour.

When we first went to Africa, we took the kind of camera that has instant pictures. They'd never seen anything like that. They were jumping up and down and screaming.

When we came off the plane in [Dakar] Africa we were greeted by a long line of African dancers. Their drums and sounds filled the air with rhythms. I was going crazy, I was screaming, "All right! I've got the rhythm... This is it! This is where I come from. The origin."

For me, it's like the dawn of civilisation. It's the first place where society existed... I guess there's that connection because it is the root of all rhythm. Everything. It's home.

The [African] rhythms are incredible. You can tell especially the way the children move. Even the little babies, when they hear the drums, they start to move.

MOVIES

Sometimes I hate to face the reality of everyday life. There's a reality in films but it's more of another life.

In the future I'll be acting and dancing in films the way it should be done, not the silly, crazy way you have to do three dance numbers in a couple of hours [for TV]. On our couple of [TV] specials I would scream about that. "This whole system is very ignorant. It is wrong, totally wrong."

Doing *The Wiz* was an incredible experience. It was always something I wanted to do, because I had always loved the movie, and always fell in love with The Scarecrow. I saw the play six times. I'll do other parts if I like the scripts, as I did with this.

What I do as The Scarecrow is, I don't think I'm smart and everything. And all through the movie I be bringing out these quotations from out of my sleeves. Aee, I'm garbage instead of straw; I'm filled with the stuff. And I'm reading these quotations from all over me about such and such: "Confucius said this." But I still think I'm ignorant.

We worked outside on the movie a lot, and it was cold, the coldest ever in New York. There were 600 dancers at the World Trade Center, all wearing costumes like swim outfits, and it was so cold a lot of them quit.

It took me three hours a day to get the make-up on, and then after I took it off, I'd look like a drug addict, with my eyes all watery and red.

It takes a long time to put on my face, but I like how different it feels. I can be in a whole other place with it. Sometimes I wear it home, and people - kids - I look out the back window of the car and let them see me. Whoa, they get frightened! They don't know who or what it is! It's a trip.

The whole thing of being in front of a camera and escaping into a whole other world is just wonderful. I have no words to describe the feeling that I had out of filming *The Wiz*. I'll never get over it.

No matter how many movie offers come to me, music will always be my number one thing, because it's inside of me and it's something that has to come out. Like when I'm going over my script, music just comes into my head, and songs, and I run to the tape recorder and put melodies on tape. Constantly. Not to wait for a piano for stuff, because I can't help it. I got to have it.

There are other deep desires that I have, especially movies. But, because of touring and recording, which I love doing, I am not able to get as involved in movies as I'd like to be. That bothers me.

My room is loaded with scripts and I just haven't had the time to look through them. Right now, what I need is a vacation.

I'd like to get more involved in movies and I'd like to direct and do movie scores. That's my

5

MICHAEL AS HE APPEARED IN ROD STEWART'S
VIDEO FOR 'THE MOTOWN SONG'.

people who aren't there. But if you capture it
on film, it's there forever. As an example, I have
been able to learn so much from watching
Charlie Chaplin.

The first time I saw *ET*, I melted through the
whole thing. The second time, I cried like crazy.
And then, in doing the narration, I felt like I was
there with them, like behind a tree or
something, watching everything that happened.

The next day I missed him a lot. I wanted to go
back to that spot I was at yesterday in the
forest. I wanted to be there.

I love *ET* because it reminds me of me.
Someone from another world coming down
and you becoming friends with them and this
person is 800 years old and he's filling you with
all kinds of wisdom and he can teach you how
to fly. That whole fantasy thing which I think is
great. I mean, who don't wanna fly?

Of all the Awards I've got, I'm most proud of
this one. **On receiving a Grammy for
Best Children's Record for the 'ET'
album in 1984.**

Cartoons are unlimited. And when you're
unlimited, it's the ultimate. Jiminy Cricket,
Pinocchio, Mickey Mouse - these are world
known characters. Some of the greatest
political figures have come to the United States
to meet them. Even people from Russia will
not leave the country without seeing
Disneyland.

It upsets me to think that [the video] 'Black Or
White' could influence any child or adult to
destructive behaviour, either sexual or violent.
I've always tried to be a good role model and
therefore, have made these changes to avoid
any possibility of adversely affecting any
individual's behaviour. I deeply regret any pain
or hurt that the final segment of 'Black Or
White' has caused children, their parents or
any other viewers.

main aim to look forward to. My greatest
experience so far [it's 1980] has been doing
The Wiz - I'll never forget that. I get lost in it
all. I am really serious and sincere about
movies.

The thing I love about films is that they
capture moments that need never be lost
and that we can constantly learn from. There
have been so many great entertainers that I
was never able to see and who have been
lost to the world. Whatever we do on stage
is just for the people in the audience at that
moment - what about the multitude of

LIFESTYLE, PSYCHOLOGY & PHILOSOPHY

I think my job is to make people happy through my music. But I do feel strange with people. All my life I've been treated differently from other people and it does make you shy.

I was a veteran before I was a teenager.

Sometimes I feel that I should be nearing the end of my life, turning 80 with people patting me on the back. That's what comes from starting so young.

I believe in God. We all do. We like to be straight, not go crazy or anything. Not to the point of losing our perspective of what you are and who you are.

I really believe that each person has a destiny from the day he is born and certain people have a thing that they're meant to do. There's a reason why the Japanese are better at technology and a reason why the Negro race are more into music - you go back to Africa and the tribes and the beating of the drums.

I'm not an angel, I know. I'm not like a Mormon or an Osmond or something where everything's straight, straight, straight. That can be silly, sometimes. It goes too far.

There's a reason God made the sunset red or purple or green. It's beautiful to look at - it's a minute of joy. There's a reason we see rainbows after rain, or a forest where the deer come out. That's wonder, that's escapism - it touches your heart and there's no danger in that. Escapism and wonder is influence.

Once when we were coming back from Africa in total darkness, we were way up and there were so many shooting stars I thought they were going to hit the plane. When you're up there where there's no smog, you almost don't see any darkness. You almost don't see any black for all the stars.

I love the whole world of dance because dancing is really the emotions through bodily movement... there's a whole psychological thing to just letting everything loose. Dancing is important, like laughing, to back off tension. Escapism... it's just great.

Every Sunday, I just have vegetable juice and I have to dance to recharge my emotional equilibrium. The fasting is good for me. It cleanses the system. The colon is like the sewage system for the body and when you fast, you flush all the impurities out. It helps to stop things like pimples and skin disorders but it's also good for you emotionally.

I've never taken drugs or had alcohol. I've never been high. I've tasted champagne but I don't drink it. When people do toasts, I just pick up the glass.

I want to live in a world with peace and without hunger. A world where mankind knows no suffering. I believe I can help achieve that goal if I stay healthy in mind and body. I believe that if I live correctly I can live to be 150.

I know what a tree feels like when the wind blows through it. And that's how I feel when I'm singing. It's wonderful.

I have learned a lot by just fooling around in private though, mostly around the house

6

MICHAEL WITH QUINCY JONES AND WHITNEY HOUSTON.

messing up the floors [dancing]. I think it's great to get up in the morning and have a big mirror in your room and cut up.

What a person says means so much. It can change a person's whole opinion of another person. I've see that happen so many times - Charlie Chaplin, Paul Robeson, Jane Fonda. All people who spoke out and then world opinion started to change on them.

My biggest fear is being misquoted. One word can be cut into a statement and change the complete meaning and colouring of what was meant. Lately, people have been twisting everything I've been saying and that's why I shy away from many interviews. I don't like to be misrepresented to my fans. I accept that I can't stop rumours. But when it's something serious and I get wrongly quoted, that's very wrong... so if I can't be quoted properly, I'd rather not be quoted at all.

I feel that I am here on earth to do a certain job and that I have only just scratched the surface and I don't want people to be given the wrong impression of me.

I've seen illusions in the air that man has never seen. We went over the North Pole and it was total dark, and you saw these big icebergs that were glowing in the night. And then I looked far out into the sky and saw purple, green and blue crystals sparkling and turning in the air. I said "What is that?" and the pilot said he didn't know, they'd only seen that once before.

I've got most of Disney's animated movies on video-tapes and when we watch them I just take-off to another planet. Oh, I could eat it, eat it.

In Disneyland, you forget about the outside world. When you walk down Main Street, you see the castle and then you see the times of the Twenties... and how do those two times fit? But they feel so good together. This is escapism.

I have all kinds of tapes and albums people would probably never think were mine. I love 'Some Girls'. Of course, [Mick Jagger] got into trouble with that one thing he said. I don't like vulgar at all. Really, at all.

I love the folk type style of music, the soul, the rhythm going out funky. I like to mix those things. And I like easy listening. I like Bread, The Carpenters. I love Stevie Wonder and The Brothers Johnson - they are smelly, they are really smelly. 'Strawberry Letter 23', that track is bad, isn't it? The lyrics are - cripes, they're so way out, they're crazy! I'm still trying to figure them out.

I don't really go out to clubs and discos at all. Sometimes you think you're going to sneak into a movie and nobody's going to see you, but as soon as you hit the door the pen and paper and pictures are there.

I just love to see the kids have a good time when the music come on. Sometime I sneak into this skating rink when they put them jams on. And you can tell when something is dirty: the kids be kicking in. Soon as there's something hot - ow! - they break out.

People came [to Studio 54] as characters and it's like going to a play. I think that's the psychological reason for the disco craze: you get to be that dream you want to be. You just go crazy with the lights and the music and you're in another world. It's very escapist.

It was the most incredible play I've ever seen. It's brilliant. Everybody should see it. **[The stage musical 'Dream Girls'.]**

There really aren't words to describe how I feel about reading. I just wish I could spend more time reading because I love it so much. I can get so lost in a book that I forget who I am and what is around me and where I am. Philosophy is my favourite subject. What's so great about reading is that there might be something that you feel or want to say and you'll come across it as a line in a book. You can sometimes read in one line in a book something you've spent a lifetime trying to work out.

I don't drive but I love cars. I like big old ones that make you feel protected. Not just some new Ford. I like the old Continentals.

I love to roller skate but I don't do any crazy sports. I didn't drive for a long time. I do now, but I'm still thinking about giving that up. I don't drive on the freeway at all, I stay in a certain area and try to be extra careful. It's like a haemophiliac who can't afford to be scratched in any way.

There's a whole psychological reason for those cartoons about good against evil. We have Superman and all those other hero people so that we can go out into life and try to be something.

Leave it up to [President Richard] Nixon. I just make records. **[Asked to comment on the energy crisis.]**

I don't know much about Watergate. It was terrible, wasn't it? I guess it was. Have you met Nixon? Is he happy? I saw him on TV last year and he looked so unhappy.

Protect me. Don't let them ask me any questions. **[An aside to an executive of LA Gear at the press conference**

announcing the $20m endorsement contract.]

I always want to know what makes good performers fall to pieces. I always try to find out. Because I just can't believe it's the same things that get them time and time again.

THE BUSINESSMAN

I care about being paid fairly for what I do. When I approach a project, I put my whole heart and soul into it. Because I really care about what I do, I put everything I can into it and expect to be paid. The guy who works should eat. It's that simple.

They demand that, and they want you to do this. They think that they own you, they think they made you. If you don't have faith, you go crazy. Like not doing interviews. If I talk, I say what's on my mind and it can seem strange to other people's ears. I'm the kind of person who will tell it all, even though it's a secret. And I know that things should be kept private.

I don't know what would make him say something like that. To hear him talk like that turns my stomach. I don't know where he gets that from. **[Michael reacting to comments by his father, Joe Jackson, about the co-managers Ron Weisner and Freddie De Mann in the fraught run-up to the Jacksons Victory tour.]**

I happen to be colour blind. I don't hire colour, I hire competence. The individual can be of any race or creed as long as I get the best. I am president of my organisation and I have the final word on every decision. Racism is not my motto. One day I strongly expect every colour to love as one family.

A JACKSON FAMILY GATHERING IN 1992.

THE JACKSON FAMILY

JOE JACKSON (FATHER)

Nobody discovered The Jacksons but their mother and father.

I was married very young and while my wife was having our nine kids I still wanted to see out my ambition to be a musician. I joined The Falcons and used to rehearse in the kitchen while the kids were crawling around the floor.

In Gary, with all the steel mills, families come in and have lots of kids, and the kids don't have anything to do, except to go to school and come home. So they learn how to sing or play some type of instrument. The kids want to better their condition, because they see their parents working every day in the mills.

We went overboard. My wife and I would fight, because I invested in new instruments that cost so much. When a woman's a good mother and finds all the money going into instruments, she doesn't like it.

I saw the potential in them being stars, big stars. And so we worked toward that goal, and they had to be talked to all the time, with a skilful hand. With an iron hand.

I rehearsed them about three years before I turned them loose. That's practically every day for at least two or three hours. When the other kids would be out on the street playing games, my boys were in the house working - trying to learn how to be something in life.

My goal was to get them on stage where they could perform with other amateurs at talent shows. It took about a year until I felt they were good enough.

It was fun, the kids liked it and it was one sure way of keeping them home and not roaming in the streets of Gary.

There's other interests in life other than just singing and dancing and The Jacksons used to play a lot of team sports. All of them, in fact, except Michael, who was strictly show business.

I had a Volkswagen bus and I bought a big luggage rack and put it on top and had everybody inside the bus. One day I noticed when I was coming out of the yard that the instruments on top of the bus were taller than the bus.

I don't want to brag, but looking at the kids I think I've done a good job. It was hard, but it sure paid off.

7

JOE AND KATHERINE JACKSON.

It always looked good, the little ones on the side and the tall one in the centre. And their voices blend well because of the family thing. There's a basic tone quality that's common to all of them.

One of my main concerns was always that they shouldn't sign away their publishing. I wanted to keep it so they could have their own publishing company. At the time they started, most groups would sign with the record company for publishing rights. I was able to avoid that and I'm very glad about that now.

Motown made the group international and that's very important. There are very big groups in the United States which are not known all over the world as we are.

My role is getting the boys out to the studios. I'm the legal guardian. They listen to me 100 per cent.

Michael would get his allowance every week from the tours. I gave him $20 and he would buy a lot of candy. He would call all his friends in the neighbourhood and Michael would give them candy.

Michael's got a good show but with the brothers it's a better show. **[Trying to sell the Victory tour.]**

Jacksons music is a type of music that the young kids like... the older people like it too... it's music for rejoicing whether you're black or white. It's for the whole world.

It's very hard. He's got a lot of people trying to get to him and bother him and he has to smile when he wants to cry. It can be rough sometimes. But that's showbiz. You either have to deal with it or get out of it.

We had some hard times, really hard times. But it looks like to me it's gotten harder. They're Number One all round the world and

everybody's taking potshots at them or taking a piece of this from them or a piece of that. People are trying to break up the family and I'm trying to hold it together.

There are a lot of leeches trying to break up the group. A lot of people whispering in Michael's ear. But we know who they are. They're only in it for the money. I was there before it started and I'll be there after it ends.

[In 1978] there was a time when I felt I needed white help in dealing with the corporate structure at CBS and thought they'd be able to help. But they never gave me the respect you expect from a business partner. **[On his relationship with Ron Weisner and Freddy De Mann.]**

As far as I'm concerned [the partnership's] over. They don't have a contract and my boys are not re-signing.

People have called me a racist... If I were a racist I wouldn't have hired a lot of people that aren't black to work for me. If I were a racist I would be somewhere else trying to start a lot of trouble.

Michael's a vegetarian... the type of vegetarian that hardly eats anything. No fish. No meat. Nuts and grapes and things of that sort and dishes that we have a cook come in to fix.

No one cooks at home. I'm the only one who eats meat. The rest only eat vegetables.

Michael never gets tired of an animal. He is like a child. In other words, he is still growing up.

Michael is religious, more so than his brothers. He is a devoted Jehovah's Witness. They were all brought up studying the Bible. My boys are very good. They're not into drugs. There's nothing wrong with having a little drink once in a while, but they don't even do that. They don't smoke... Michael's as thin as a razor.

KATHERINE JACKSON (MOTHER)

Ever since Michael was very young he seemed different to me from the rest of the children. I don't believe in reincarnation, but you know how babies move unco-ordinated? He never moved that way. When he danced, it was like he was an older person.

It was sort of frightening. [Michael] was so young. He didn't go out and play very much. So if you want me to tell you the truth, I don't know where he got it. He just knew.

You know children. If they don't have TV to watch then they have to do other things.

Michael is pretty stable. I think it's his raising. We used to talk to the boys about getting big heads. None of them is better than anyone else. One might have a little more talent, but that doesn't make you better.

Michael isn't gay. It's against his religion. It's against God. The Bible speaks against it.

A lot of people think they're really Michael. They sign autographs as Michael, they smoke, have liquor and Michael doesn't do that.

Every time I'd go to a concert, I'd worry because sometimes the girls would get on stage and I'd have to watch them tearing at Michael. He was so small and they were so big.

Michael used to say when he wrote, he'd write for everyone even though the music business would list it as rhythm and blues because of him being black.

It's just a job. Other people might be doctors and lawyers but Michael entertains because maybe that's what he can do best. That doesn't mean he's better.

[Joe] always walks around with a "kick me" sign on his back. **[Katherine's opinion of her husband, according to daughter LaToya.]**

JERMAINE

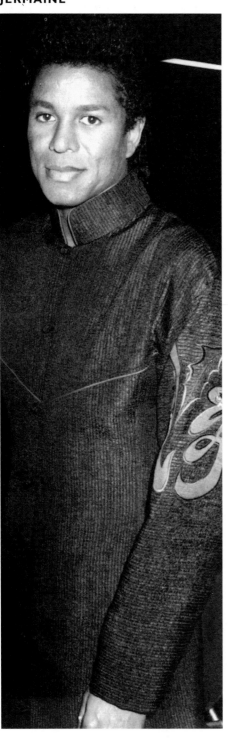

In The Beginning

Those days were such fun. I remember after our first show we got five dollars to split seven ways.

We were all very serious about the business and of course we already knew how to act on stage before we joined Motown. I think we were probably the only group in this business to do what we did as quickly as we did, and that's a great feeling for us.

We were treading the boards long before Motown. I was ten when we started doing the Apollo in Harlem and the big night clubs. I never knew any different but I'm glad to see my own kids grow in a more normal way. It really came to me when I first watched them opening their presents at Christmas and getting so excited - it's something I never had because my family were Jehovah's Witnesses so we didn't get to celebrate Christmas.

When The Jackson 5 started getting success [Motown] kept us out of the public's eye on purpose as a strategy, to make a mystique, so we were never allowed to visit friends or go to a ball game. And that's bad for kids.

They covered every aspect of our life and behaviour. A team worked on our career development. They told us what to say, what we shouldn't say, how to be polite and explained that conduct and behaviour was always very important.

We were shown how to look. Some of my brothers needed dental work and that was all taken care of. Then we had set situations like talk shows. Every talk show host basically asks the same questions so we ran through these because nobody wanted to look stupid. We were all very young at the time - I was 13 - and we wanted to make it. This seemed the best way of going about it. It was fun.

They considered me as the first teen black sex symbol. I was at the prime age. I was sixteen. So they wanted to hear more from me by myself. Those [first Motown solo] albums were pretty good because I had my first number one record by myself ['Daddy's Home'].

We were the two lead singers and Dad always sent us to bed early because he wanted our voices to get plenty of rest. So Michael became a very special person to me. I'm the person who advises him. And he listens to me. Michael looks up to me because I talk straight to him.

1973
Michael and I [write] a lot of songs. We're doing one now for Glen Campbell. We like his style and the kind of songs he does and that's the sort of things we write. We were really happy when he said he'd like to do one of ours.

I'm doing some producing on Michael now. We have a studio at home now, my father did it for us. Sid Fein, who is a big arranger for television

shows and movies, is doing an arrangement of one of my songs for Michael. It's about a bird.

We try to create our own personalities so the people know us as individuals within the group. People know our names, they're always calling out for one of us. I'm the romantic, Tito goes funky. Jackie blows the harmonica and gives us the sweet melodies. We all have certain songs.

Split
Usually, when you hear of somebody going someplace else, at least you would sit down and have a discussion about it. The first thing I saw was all the [Epic] contracts with their names on them, so they had already left. They figured by them signing ahead of time I would go ahead and sign. So that's why I'm by myself now.

It was a decision I took myself. I had to think of my own career and after weighing everything up it seemed obvious to me I'd be better off all-round sticking with Motown. The company has always been good to me.

A lot of people say [my decision] had a lot to do with my marriage to the daughter [Hazel] of the owner and chairman of the board of Motown [Berry Gordy].That didn't have anything to do with it. I sort of felt this break-up coming along but no-one would come out and tell me that they were leaving. I said to my wife one day, "If I had to leave would that affect our marriage?" And she said, "No, because we got married to live a personal life not a record business life". Success wasn't the reason I started caring for her. It was just simple boyfriend and girlfriend.

It wasn't my decision to be solo. This is not what I wanted to do. But I had no choice. My brothers had signed elsewhere before I knew it and so it caught me by surprise.

To this very day I can say that Michael never wanted to leave. But he was too young to voice a strong opinion, to say, "No father, I am not going. I'm very happy where I am".

I guess a lot of it had to do with the fact that we were very spoiled. Our success didn't start overnight because we were working in a lot of clubs before we came to Motown. But the first professional record we ever recorded was platinum. It went straight to the top. That happened six or seven times in a row.

When all of a sudden that cools, one would probably get nervous and say, "Well, what's wrong?" and you'd say, "Well, the record company's not doing something right so maybe we ought to go elsewhere". But everybody, they're hot for a while, then they cool off. As big as The Beatles were, they cooled off and then they split up and they had individual success.

Michael and I are very close and we were even closer then because we were always together. We shared rooms together the first time we came to England, we were the two that stayed together because we just have a certain rapport. Now, we're still very close but it's a distant closeness. It's like if I'm way over here, he knows that I'm still thinking about him and he's thinking about me but it's not the same. If we were both in this room we would just joke and laugh about something silly. Those are the things that I remember and that I try to express in these lyrics [to 'We Can Put It Back Together', a track off Jermaine's 1979 album 'Let's Get Serious'].

1979

We all thought we were right in what we were doing and the one good thing is that we have all been successful since. There is still a demand for us to all get back together again one day and when we do it will be a special day for all of us, believe me. Right now, there are legal reasons why it can't happen but we are still a very close family and, in fact, they have invited me to go with them on their next tour.

I miss being on stage with them because there was nothing that we couldn't do on-stage, no end to what we could do together as a group. I just feel it's gonna happen and when it does happen, I'm gonna be so excited... and much happier too.

'We Can Put It Back Together' is a very important song, very special to me. This song makes me cry sometimes, because it's about my brothers. I put in one word to tie in a double meaning about a marriage that didn't make it but basically it's about my brothers.

Early 1980s
My brothers and I have been talking. It's the first time we've met in five or six years. We're probably going to be doing a big tour together. It's going to be really exciting, because we're going to be doing a lot of the old stuff.

My philosophy of going out on the road is I want to do it the way we did when we first started. When we were first introduced, everything was planned. People didn't see us until after three number one records so the demand was there.

All the family sees each other every day to go running or visit the parents. [On] our mother's birthday all the grandchildren will be doing a Jackson 5 routine and Michael will be making a speech on What Mothers Are For.

1983
The group was reunited on stage, with Jermaine clearly in tears, for Motown's 25th Anniversary celebrations and concert, an emotional moment. Yes it was. It was very emotional for me, the whole evening was emotional for us all. It really felt like being home again.

1984
A Jermaine-Michael duet, 'Tell Me I'm Not Dreaming', was to be lifted off Jermaine's 'Dynamite' album on Arista

MICHAEL WITH BROOKE SHIELDS

but CBS, Michael's label, blocked its release as a single.
This would probably be my only Number One ever but I can't put it out. Michael okayed it three times but he says there's nothing he can do. It's surprising because when Michael got hurt, I was the only brother **[CBS Records boss Walter Yetnikoff]** called, trying to find Michael. He didn't call Marlon. He didn't call Jackie. He called me and I'm not even at his company. If [Michael] says it's out of his hands, then it's out of his hands. But there's another side to it: understanding how much leverage you have after selling 30 million albums. **[The track was eventually released as a B-side, in a version without Michael's vocal.]**

It's so good that we've actually done a making-of-the-video video - just like 'Thriller'. **[On promoting 'When The Rain Begins To Fall', Jermaine's duet with Pia Zadora, directed by Bob Giraldi, whose previous credits included 'Say Say Say', Paul McCartney and Michael.]**

Rockwell's a nice guy, he's Berry's [Gordy] son. Do you think the single ['Somebody's Watching Me'] sold because of us - Michael and I? I thought it was a hit as soon as I heard it, without our vocals on it.

Michael and I have always been close and he still needs a lot of loving. He is under strain right now, so many people want him to do so many things. Half of the stories printed about him are untrue, and this does upset him. He tries not to keep himself to himself but he's not a lonely person. He lives with my parents in Encino with the youngest member of my family. It's real difficult for him to lead a normal life, and even to go outside of the house's grounds is difficult because he gets mobbed. Entertaining is the only life he's known and we all give thanks we've been successful.

He's worked hard and as much as we were all surprised at the way his career has gone, it couldn't have happened to a more deserving guy. We're all delighted for him and we all support him. He can handle his career all right, don't worry about that, because he knows exactly where he's going and what he wants to do. He's got a very shrewd business head.

He eats just as much as the rest of us but burns it all off.

Michael knows what he wants, and when it's time for him to be firm and businesslike that kid switches completely and handles his affairs very well.

Michael isn't the loner that everybody thinks he is - and he certainly isn't gay. He has lovers and dates a great deal but people just don't know where he goes.

Michael is having an affair with Brooke Shields and sees her a lot. Every time I talk to him about her he smiles and seems to be very, very happy. I keep saying to him "Do I hear wedding bells, Michael?" and he breaks into a big grin. But he dates other women, including a former Miss Universe and Tatum O'Neal. He's also very close to Diana Ross but he isn't obsessed with her.

Michael is a Jehovah's Witness and believes in his religion but he's not a fanatic. He's a very warm, loving person who needs lots of affection. He often says to me "With all the hit records and millions and millions rolling in, there comes a time when you've got to say, I'm a person as well. I'm a human being just like everyone else and I want to enjoy myself. It's great entertaining people and giving them joy and love, but what about the Michael inside?"

Michael's very shy, quiet and sensitive. He's also a perfectionist. He always wants the best and he'll go out and buy it. But early in the morning, dressed in disguise, he loves to go to swop shops where he can trade and bargain.

MARLON

We would do a show somewhere on Sunday night, we'd get home at three in the morning, then we'd have to get up at eight to go to school. That was rough.

I believe people jumped on The Jacksons [Victory album and tour] as a reaction to Michael's success. They said 'Victory' was a flop because it sold three million records. Three million records are hard to sell. Just because Michael sold forty million of 'Thriller' what we did suddenly didn't mean anything.

[He is proud of Michael's success but] it can get to you when everyone asks us what he's up to. Michael is my brother, but I don't know his every move - I'm too busy running my own life. Michael hasn't said no to doing another group album when he finishes his solo album.

The family had the feeling ['Thriller'] would sell. After all, 'Off The Wall' had done eight million

so we figured he would at least match that. Three years ago it was hard to sell a million, so you can't suddenly expect to sell thirty million every time out. People just don't have the money to support that again so soon. But I do feel that since our last [studio] album did about 2.5 million we'll do well over that.

We were looking for someone with integrity, experience, imagination and a knowledge of both black and white audiences... someone who could handle the unusual. **[Frank Russo and Danny O'Donovan appointed co-promoters of Victory tour. Relationship lasted three weeks; Russo later sued The Jacksons for $40m.]**

After we did the Victory tour I went to the company [Epic] and told them I wanted to do a solo album, they said they wanted a group album first, that maybe I could do a solo project after we did that, so that's when I decided I should officially leave the group. **[Marlon finally cut a solo album, 'Baby Tonight' for Capitol in 1987.]**

I've been singing with the group all my life. In 1963, when I was a kid I remember doing eight shows at the Apollo. At some point, you want to reach for singular instead of group goals. There's family and there's business. This is business.

The only way [my name] helps me in my solo career is, I knew the people would put the needle on the wax. And if it wasn't happening, that was it. No more.

When you've got five brothers, everyone's in charge of everything. You don't care as much. You drop the dribble, someone else will pick it up. But now it's just me. I love it. I love the challenge.

Out of all the family, he tries harder than anyone. He has tremendous integrity and courage and needed both to fill the gap when Jermaine left. **[Michael on Marlon.]**

RANDY

I love [Europe]. I love the architecture and the old monuments, the whole historical thing because there the history goes back thousands of years whereas in America it's only hundreds. Michael is into the same things over there too.

[Michael loved *The Wiz*]... he knows and loves Diana and that made it so much easier for him. She's like a sister. He loved the original film and he loved the play. He saw it when he didn't know he was going to do the movie. He saw it about thirteen times.

Randy is multi-talented and can play virtually any instrument. He's like a flower that opens during the day and closes at night. He is also a talented writer and although he has a slight handicap from his car accident in 1980, he's holding on and is real strong. **[Michael on Randy.]**

JACKIE

It's the quickest getaway in show business. **[From stage to limousine in six seconds.]**

Michael and Jermaine were the first to perform solo but we all knew we would. We want to show what we can do individually. Michael's records all sold over a million and Jermaine's album is doing very well. It's something to live up to. My own album is in a different bag from what we do as a group. It's older, for instance, more like The Stylistics or Dionne Warwick. As you grew old your taste in music changes, old rock and roll is coming back but my album is heavily into strings and ballads.

We've made a tradition of breaking songs on television. You get to more people that way, it seems a good alternative to test markets.

In our block there were a lot of groups competing. Every time there was a talent show everyone would come to try for the trophy. Deniece Williams was one of them, and Kellee Patterson.

Nobody ever took lessons. Music was just a family thing and we used to come home from school and rehearse. There was just nothing else to do.

[Michael] was so energetic that at five years old he was like a leader. We saw that. So we said, "Hey, Michael, you be the lead guy". The audience ate it up. He was into those James Brown things at the time. The speed was the thing. He would see somebody do something and he could do it right away.

What we do is record a lot of songs and the producers and staff at Motown pick the best ones.

[Fan hysteria is] not too good because sometimes you lose the groove when you have to stop the performance for a few minutes.

Motown are a great company. Our contract expired and we just wanted to move on and do other things. Motown were a little slow in coming up with the right kind of contract at that particular time. We couldn't wait around and so we moved right away to the people that had it.

When we record in our [24 track home] studio we just cut. If the record comes out and is played in the disco, that's great. But we don't record disco, we record dancing music.

They want to be stars themselves. Everybody wants to play a very, very important part and feel important. Don King's that way. Irving Azoff's the same way. Sometimes I can't believe it. It's like power games they're playing. I know it. We all know it. They must know it. **[On 'advisers' on the Victory tour.]**

Jackie has always been the protection on the road for everyone and keeping all the family together when my father's not there. He's a good element and chemistry for the group and he's a born organiser. Because of him, things get done. **[Michael on Jackie.]**

TITO

I think the first paying gig was at a place called Mr Lucky's. We got $5 for all of us; we made more money from people pitching money from the floor. We knew something was happening when we started winning the talent shows.

Sure we have arguments but very seldom and they're all in brotherly love. We wouldn't be a family if we didn't. Too much happiness is no good anyway.

When a group's contract runs out, they negotiate better deals. Our contract at Motown wasn't up to par compared with other groups of our standing at the time, so we felt that it was time for us to either get a better contract or move on. The company that came up with the best deal was CBS. More freedom had a lot to do with it, our own publishing, writing, producing.

After all our years in the business there is still room for us to expand our horizons. The year we left Motown, I was set to do my first solo album... but I never got around to doing mine. So even if my songs don't make 'Victory', I see myself recording an album and showing my vocal abilities.

It's always the outside people who cause the problems. **[Verdict on the Victory tour.]**

Tito is very quiet and soft but he can be really strong when necessary. He's always there when we need him and manages to project an inner calm which is vital within a family unit. **[Michael on Tito.]**

JANET

[The youngest of the Jackson children, Janet was closest to Michael. At one time, she sat in on his interviews, whispering the questions into his ear. He'd whisper answers to her, she'd pass them on to the interviewer.]

He said that, out of everyone in the family, we're the two that think most alike... he gave a lot of advice. He inspires me.

Growing up in my family we were very sheltered and my parents made it very convenient for us to have everything we wanted. Such as a movie theatre.

We always used to watch all the old MGM musicals. I was always Cyd Charisse, Michael was Fred Astaire and LaToya was Ginger Rogers.

Of course, it helped me a lot, being a Jackson. I've never had to audition for anything.

I remember the time he only got one Grammy nomination for 'Off The Wall'. He was so disappointed. His eyes started to water. I felt so bad for him, but he finally said, "You watch the next album I do. You watch, I'll show them."

When 'Thriller' came, I was so envious. It was so incredible. I was so happy for him but it was like, "Why can't that be me? That's what I want to do". That's what inspired me to do 'Control'.

[To suggestion that her voice sounded like Michael's.] Oh well, that's what you get from being in the same family. I can't hear it, I honestly can't.

This one girl got so upset when her friend told her that rumour [that Michael was gay] that she jumped out of the window. I think she died.

Michael is very quiet, very shy. When you see him on stage, it's like two different people. There's something inside everybody that's dying to get out. That's what happens on stage.

Every time I see my brother perform I get so excited. I got a copy of Michael's show on video and I studied it.

I've worked so hard to find my own identity that [duetting with Michael] would seem to be self-defeating.

I've studied the best. Michael Jackson, who was just down the hall. I'm not saying that because he's my brother. I really feel he is the best. I saw how hard he works, his ambition. It's so strange to read things about him because people just don't understand Michael much.

It's difficult to stay in touch but we try. Mum knows where everyone is. We still need each other. Friends are important, but family...

Janet and I are very close because we're both silly at times, but she is a talented singer and a serious actress. She will come through and make a very special contribution to life. People will see something in Janet that they didn't realise was there. **[Michael on Janet.]**

BERRY GORDY

MOTOWN & PRODUCERS

BERRY GORDY, Motown's founder

Michael was a born star. He was nine years old when the Jacksons auditioned for me. He was the classic example of understanding everything. He watched me like a hawk. He had a depth that was so vast, it was just incredible.

[He sang] with a certain amount of pain - he was a kid, so where did he get that pain from? I decided I would pattern his style after Frankie Lymon. I came up with the melody for the first song ['I Want You Back'] we released on the Jackson 5 myself. The kid inspired me so much.

We had a very close relationship. When I was moving to California I decided to move him out with me. They had their band, and we would put them in a house and they would get kicked out. Finally, I said "OK, you move into my house" because I wanted them to rehearse.

[Michael] is the greatest performer alive today.

Of course I worry about him and all the pressures that must be on him but he is so strong mentally and physically that he can handle it.

FREDDIE PERREN, Motown producer, one of The Corporation team

I never saw any songs he wrote but I always knew he could. There was an instrumental hit out, 'Love Is Blue'. He came in one day and asked me about this section of the song he found interesting. I showed it to him on the piano. He couldn't play but he was able to learn his part and would sit there picking it out. There is a certain talent that goes with songwriting and I could see he had it. Motown just didn't encourage it in performers. At Motown the producer was king.

JERRY MARCELLINO, Motown co-producer with Mel Larson

We did ['Rockin' Robin'] as a kind of a lark because nostalgia was happening then. It sold 2.5 million copies, so they decided to let us be producers.

In the studio, we don't rehearse [The Jackson 5]. We give them the track and cut it then do background and lead vocals right there.

MEL LARSON, Motown co-producer with Jerry Marcellino.

Too much rehearsal will take away from their creative ability. The spontaneous feeling is more important when you're stretching out a tune. They can hear a song once and sing it back to you.

WALTER SCHARF, composer of the music to 'Ben'

[Michael was] meticulous about everything, almost to a fault. Very disciplined. I think it's marvellous to be like that at that age - to have that kind of knowledge and feeling toward your work.

LEON HUFF, with KENNY GAMBLE, producers and writers on two Jacksons' albums after the split with Motown.

We had a lot of fun working with them. What we were trying to do was to broaden their audience. They were in a natural period of transition that reflected their growth. But I believe the experience was good all round and for both parties. At the time, we were happy with the product - it sounded good to us. We had them all singing, that was new. I think everything worked out for the best. We contributed towards helping them to be able to produce themselves and that helped their growth.

8

QUINCY JONES, producer of 'Off The Wall', 'Thriller' and 'Bad'.

Michael is like an '80s Sammy Davis Jr. He's the best of Broadway, Disneyland, Vegas, pop, rock 'n' roll, R&B, all of that. He knows what Olivier does, what Brando does, what Astaire does, what James Brown does. He knows.

He's taken us right up there where we belong. Black music had to play second fiddle for a long time, but its spirit is the whole motor for pop. Michael has connected with every soul in the world.

[They first met at Sammy Davis Jr's house when Michael was 12 and met again on the set of *The Wiz*, 1978, Jackson co-starring as The Scarecrow, Jones doing the soundtrack.]
It was interesting that the first long time we spent together he was doing more acting than singing. There was this side to him that I had never seen before and was different from the teeny-bopper young image that he had.

His performance in *The Wiz* is just mind-boggling even for an oldtimer, let alone someone who's taking his first shot at film.

I started to see this disciplined, curious mind. He'd come in at five o'clock to do make-up and they'd start shooting at seven. He knew everybody's lines, every part, he never complained. I saw this incredible depth and musicianship in him and when he called me up to ask if I knew anybody who would produce his album, I said I'd do it.

In a family situation, you're dealing with kids that come from the same mother and father. You know, it's in the genes. The way their voices melt together has a unique quality because their voices all have a certain element in

STEVIE WONDER, QUINCY JONES, DIONNE WARWICK, MICHAEL, AND LIONEL RICHIE.

common like in the tone and texture. Also, you're dealing with a situation where they've been doing it together since they were babies.

We call Michael Jackson 'Smelly' because he's so polite we can't even get him to say the word funky. He's the purest product in America today.

In the studio we don't treat him like a star. He gets his [voice] coach in to warm him up and then he's ready to hit it. He does his little dances on each take.

He reminds me of the kid in Truffaut's *Enfant Sauvage*: inspired but shy. He always sings with his back turned in the studio.

We had everything in the can for 'Thriller' and we were about to leave the studio. I played the tapes a few more times and I just didn't get that feeling. I told Michael that he had to write some stronger material. Over the next few days he wrote 'Billie Jean' and 'Beat It'.

I could never believe that a song with the beat and lyric content of 'Billie Jean' could be conceived by Michael Jackson. He hasn't had a lot of romantic relationships, if any, but it is very powerful stuff.

Michael has always been isolated. I'd go to his house and there were always 30 girls outside all the time. They even got in the house. One day there was one lying out by the pool, nobody knew who she was. I think she was the inspiration for 'Billie Jean'. Michael just said, "It's been like that all my life."

I guess [Michael] put more into 'Bad' than any of the other albums. The other albums he was only involved with the songs he wrote. I asked him to write all the songs on 'Bad' and even though he wrote something like 30 songs, we still used two outside songs. The more he writes the more he gets involved. So he was very involved in 'Bad'.

Everything on that stage comes from his mind: the lighting, the dance, everything. He's an amazing little guy. He has this wild uniqueness and originality that mark him out as one of the best performers I've ever seen. Maybe the best.

He's been in show business since he was five years old so he doesn't look at things in the same way you and I do. He sees the world through different eyes.

Michael has to go and see some children at a hospital and someone says, "There is this oxygen tent to sustain life." It's fascinating and he wants to see it. He gets in it, says "I could live 150 years in this" and the story gets out. Michael is not going to be a Howard Hughes figure, lingering on life. That's not him.

People take him for a simpleton with a head full of silly songs but he's a complex young man, curious about everything, who wants to go further and further. He behaves like an adolescent and at the same time like a wise old philosopher. I feel kind of responsible for him but at times it's him who plays the role of father.

Michael just loves animals, so do a lot of people. Bubbles is a hell of a lot of fun - though I'm not too crazy about his python. The chimp's got better table manners than most musicians I know.

I think Michael's whole situation has been grossly exaggerated and taken out of context. I'm not saying that Michael is your average guy next door. See, when somebody gets that big, especially a black artist and there's never been a black artist as big as Michael, that's part of the price you pay. I'd love to get him a little wilder and have some fun.

I love Michael. I know Michael like I know my own son. There's a part of me that will always be a part of Michael as long as we live, and vice versa. But no one said we were meant to be bound at the hip.

I would love to hear [Michael] produce an album on himself. We don't have anything to prove any more. We've already done it. I feel like whatever that was about, we did it in the '80s. This is the '90s now. It's time to do something else.

He is the most on-the-case person I've ever met. He can appear shy and fragile but he has a strong vision and that's what is unique about him. He can maintain innocence and still have the wisdom of a 70-year-old man.

COURTNEY SALE ROSS, film producer of Listen Up: The Lives Of Quincy Jones.

[Michael agreed to appear in the film but insisted on his own lighting crew and would say only "I love you Quincy". Ross demurred. A compromise audio interview took place in a darkened room.]
He gave a great interview. He said at the beginning that he would answer only three questions. As one thing led to another I said, "Can I ask you another question?" He said, "Oh. That would be really nice".

Control is a big issue for Michael. There's a lot of anxiety for him about how it's going to be and how to control it. Once he got there, we saw the side of Michael that I've seen and

everybody who knows him falls in love with, the side that's very sweet and wonderful. That's the side that came out once we got him in there without any managers or lawyers or anybody else.

ROD TEMPERTON, songwriter for many tracks on 'Off The Wall' and 'Thriller'.

When I first worked with Quincy, which was the Michael Jackson album ['Off The Wall'], he called me up one day in New York and said, "I need you to write some songs for Michael Jackson and Rufus. Can you do it?" I said, "No, I'm in the middle of a Heatwave project." Finally, he wrangled out of me that I would do one song for each artist.

[He gave Michael three to choose from.]
The one I thought would be their choice was 'Off The Wall'. I tried to find out about Michael's character. I knew he loved Charlie Chaplin and I thought 'Off The Wall' was a nice thing for Michael. That was the A song. 'Rock With You' was a rhythm section idea I'd had before. I thought I'd go with this one too because he's good at handling very melodic things. The third one ['Burn This Disco Out'] was written at that time as well.

I finished the [Heatwave] session at five Saturday morning in New York, dashed back to the hotel, grabbed my things, caught the flight to LA, got there, car took me straight to the studio, they pushed me in and we cut the three rhythm tracks completely blind in two six-hour sessions. At the end of it I said, "Q, you haven't said much. What do you think of them? Which one do you want?" He said, "What are you talking about? We want all three!" He'd conned me! So I flew back to New York to be with Heatwave in the studio the next morning and had to frantically start writing all three lyrics to go back the following weekend and cut the vocals. [He did] and got in with Michael and he

MICHAEL WITH GUITARIST JENNIFER BATTEN DURING THE DANGEROUS TOUR IN 1992.

rehearsed the lead melody and then overnight he learnt the lyrics and on the Sunday he came in and cut the whole background vocals and lead melodies in one afternoon. So those three songs were completed in 24 hours of recording. That's what I mean about it being a magic situation.

At the beginning I was absolutely frightened to death. The first day I went on the session, I arrived and there were all these top LA session musicians. Quincy kinda pushes me from behind and says, "Fellas, this is Rod Temperton. Hit it, Rod, I'll be in the box". I guess that was the luckiest thing that ever happened to me.

When we came out of the studio and listened to the whole album before it was ever played to the record company, we all just looked at each other and smiled "This is happening!" I was surprised it did as many as it did. I guess it's one of the biggest black albums for a long time. I felt pretty positive it would be a platinum album. I think everybody was.

Bruce Swedien, engineer on 'Off The Wall', 'Thriller', 'Bad' and 'Dangerous'.

[Quincy Jones] listened to a thousand songs or some astronomical number to get the nine songs that eventually were on the album ['Thriller']. I've never seen Quincy so into anything. Ever. In all our years we've worked together.

It's a small mock-up of what the songs will appear like. At that stage they try different counter melodies and different vocal registers and make it work for Michael. Quincy does this on everything. **[Jones' musical "Polaroid" snaps.]**

If you listen to the strings [on the "Thriller" album] you'll swear you're in Carnegie Hall. The recording of it is as legitimate and straightforward as a classical recording.

When we do vocals we usually start at noon. During that period, every day that Michael records, he's at his vocal coach's place at 8.30 in the morning. So when he comes in, he's ready to go.

All this stuff about Michael being a weirdo, it's a pile of goddam... I've recorded a whole lot of these pop musicians and this guy's the straightest of the goddam lot. OK, Michael's got a few minor quirks but everybody in California does. OK, he has some animals. But we're all crazy about animals. We got a 200lb Great Dane that comes to the studios every day to keep Michael's chimp company. OK, so he has his nose changed a bit. That's just normal in LA. I've looked in every room in that mansion of his for the oxygen tent he's supposed to sleep in and it ain't in his bedroom, it ain't anywhere.

These older ladies Michael hangs out with. It's just a mothering thing. He's so shy he hasn't had too much experience of young ladies. He tells my wife, Bea, he wants to get married and have ten kids. His producer, Quincy Jones, and I have been trying to give him a lot of help in that direction. He'll be OK in the end.

One thing that is true about Michael is he's got principles. You can never get him to swear. We've been trying for ten years. He gets real embarrassed.

Michael Jackson is both the youngest and the oldest and wisest man I've ever met. I'd be proud to have that kid as my son any day.

Michael started [on 'Dangerous'] the day we finished 'Bad'. The next day he was in doing demos.

Michael's desire [for 'Dangerous'] was to present something very street that the young people will be able to identify with. That was a conscious decision on his part.

If ['Dangerous'] sold 100 million, I don't think he'd be totally satisfied but he'd hold still for that.

TEDDY RILEY, co-writer and producer of seven tracks on 'Dangerous'.

[Michael] told me I was the best producer out there. He has so many songs that could be on the album. If mine make it, great. If not, at least I got to work with Michael Jackson.

[Earlier, Riley had produced The Jacksons' '2300 Jackson Street'.]
The difference between Michael and his brothers is Michael knows what he wants and the others don't. Michael prepares, he practises at home, he sleeps with the tape on. And then, when he gets to the studio he can just knock it out.

We didn't want to sound like another 'Thriller'. We wanted to top it, even though that's impossible. If 'Dangerous' doesn't sell more than 'Bad', even with the recession we're having, then I don't feel that it's better.

He wanted to work on grooves. So I came in with ten grooves. He liked them all.

Michael likes to listen even louder than me. And he jams! Only way you know your music is right is if he's dancing all over the studio.

We used a variety of drum machines [throughout 'Dangerous'] but we compressed all our snares to make 'em pop. On ['She Drives Me Wild'] the whole percussion track is motor sounds: trucks, cars starting, cars screeching, motorcycles revving car horns. Even the bass is a car horn. I made the samples myself. We even sampled Michael's tiger.

Thank God for Michael Jackson. He has helped me so much. These songs on 'Dangerous' will determine how my career will be. I was worried that people were getting tired of my music. I don't know what the future holds, but whatever happens I'll always have this.

Everybody tells me ['Dangerous'] is a great album, that they love what I'm doing with Michael. I like that; that's cool. But I don't have an ego about it. I just say thank you and be on my way.

I sorta wish I'd been able to do the things I've done for Michael Jackson with [Riley's group] Guy. If we'd had the same discipline then maybe we'd be at the top.

Michael does call his family. All this rumour about him not calling anybody, not answering the calls - come on. I've been there plenty of times when Michael was talking to his Mom, and I've spoken to his Mom and I've spoken to Janet. It's a bunch of crap.

[Jermaine's 'Word To The Badd!!'] was a desperate attempt for fame.

We anticipated a lot of people saying a lot of stuff about Michael. Hammer going after Michael and Jermaine going after Michael. We anticipated that. That's why we wrote songs like 'Trippin' ['Why You Wanna Trip On Me'] and 'Jam'. We know people are after him, people are talking about him. But we didn't get too direct, we didn't say anybody's name. Cause when you're too direct, it gets boring.

I'm quite sure that if Michael could have done it all over again, he would not have done that. But there's no turning back. Once you change your description, you can't turn back. You can't get your own face or your own skin back again. But he is still Michael Jackson, he is still the talented man that everybody grew up on.

BILL BOTTRELL, co-producer on 'Dangerous'.

He doesn't like to be negative. He has his own indications and you just learn what they are. Walking out of the room is one way.

He hears the sound and the whole arrangement of the song in his head... this is generally the way it is. He fills in the lyrics later. He hums things. He can convey it with his voice like nobody. Not just singing the song's lyrics but he can convey a feeling in a drum part or a synthesizer part.

That piece of music, the beginning part that Slash plays on, was first recorded at Michael's house. Michael asked me to dig it out of the vault in August of '89. He had in mind to use it as the intro to 'Black Or White'. It took a long time before we got Slash on it.

BOBBY COLOMBY, co-executive producer of The Jacksons' 'Destiny', former Blood, Sweat and Tears drummer and music reporter on CBS.

I haven't been around Michael much since he was 19 but I know that then he was very upset at the idea that any kids might perceive him as gay. He's very graceful, and he has this high-pitched voice and so inevitably there are people who think he might be gay. I saw no indication of it. So anyway, if that question came up I would say "No".

He's like any kid next door that became a lead singer when he was five... anyone who has been treated as a meal ticket all his life... anyone who is by nature an entertainer. What may seem fantasy to us isn't fantasy to Michael. If he wants to have lunch with Sophia Loren or Elizabeth Taylor, it's no problem. And because he's living that fantasy, it's no longer fantastic. So is it fair to condemn him if he then tries to find some other fantasy which isn't everyone's normal idea of a fantasy?

He's surrounded by people who say "Michael, great idea! Let's roll with it!" When you've already been perceived as God on vinyl, God on tape, and now God on CD, it's always going to be difficult to top yourself.

Nothing is sacred. Songs are songs. If they help sell things like Nike, fine. Lots of people probably think running shoes are more sacred than The Beatles. **[Michael had bought The Beatles publishing and allowed Nike to use The Beatles' 'Revolution' in an advertisement. The surviving Beatles were outraged.]**

THE GIRL IS MINE
BY MICHAEL AND PAUL

STEVEN SPIELBERG.

VIDEO DIRECTORS, MUSICIANS & MANAGEMENT

STEVEN SPIELBERG, director of ET, Close Encounters Of The Third Kind, The Color Purple, Jaws, Empire of the Sun and three Indiana Jones films.
If ET hadn't come to Elliott's house, he would have come to Michael's.

He's sort of like a fawn in a burning forest. It's a nice place where Michael comes from. I wish we could all spend some time in his world.

Michael is one of the last living innocents who is in complete control of his life. I've never seen anybody like Michael. He's an emotional star child.

He's in full control. Sometimes he appears to other people to be sort of wavering on the fringes of twilight, but there is great conscious forethought behind everything he does. He's very smart about his career and the choices he makes. I think he's definitely a man of two personalities.

JOHN LANDIS, director of, among others, An American Werewolf In London, The Blues Brothers, Trading Places, National Lampoon's Animal House and of the 'Thriller' and 'Black Or White' videos.
With Michael, as with any superstar, reality and fantasy are totally confused. It's very difficult to remain sane. I think he's doing the right thing by cutting himself off from the press because the press tends to write what it wants anyway. But I tell you, I really like him a lot. He's very smart, he's a very nice man.

Michael's a real celebrity magnet. I remember looking over at one of these giant seven foot speakers Michael was having the song played through, and Nancy Reagan was standing right in front of it. All I had to yell was "Playback!" and that would have been it.

He's taken a lot more control of his own life.

When I made 'Thriller' I dealt with thousands of managers and record people and all this stuff and it's pretty clear to me that Mike makes his own decisions now.

He has a lot more pressure on him now. There's a lot more jealousy. Michael, you know, is an old pro. People still think of Michael Jackson as little Michael Jackson but you're talking about someone who was on the Ed Sullivan show, I mean he was making live performances and working hard from the time he was little.

He really has a very strong sense of responsibility, a strong sense of showmanship.

Michael wanted ['Black Or White'] to be even more sexually explicit... It wasn't so much what Michael was doing but the juxtaposition of simulated masturbation with the violence. And, of course, the fact that it was Michael. I don't know that we discussed his intention. It was simply "I'd like to do this" and me giving him what he wanted.

He was under extreme pressure to deliver his album ['Dangerous']. He had the entire Rising Sun on his ass. They had to drag it out of him.

BOB GIRALDI, director of 'Say, Say, Say' and the Pepsi commercial.
He's absolutely a perfectionist. Michael is the kind of person who surrounds himself with the best talent available: the best director, the best cameraman, the best hair and make-up people, the best wardrobe. He can tell if you're lightweight, and he'll move on to someone else right off the bat.

COLIN CHILVERS, director of the 'Smooth Criminal' video.
I expected it to be difficult, and it was. Michael's a perfectionist, and when you are trying to break new ground and working with special

9

effects it's inevitable that there is frustration. The main difficulty is that Michael is so busy. There is always something dragging him from one meeting to another. I don't know how he handles it as well as he does. For anyone working with Michael, the greatest frustration is always going to be getting enough access to him.

LAURA GROSS, writer/deviser of TV special Michael Jackson - Rock's Thriller.
He was definitely a little shy but I wouldn't say withdrawn. All the time he was talking to me he was sketching on a little pad - faces, little pairs of legs, all kind of whimsical. At the end I asked him if I could have the sketch and he said, "No, but I'll trade you for the button you're wearing". It was just a little fun button with the name of a group on it so I handed it over and he signed his sketch and gave it to me. I'm told it's probably worth at least $5,000.

People are saying he's greater than Presley or The Beatles but I think it's too early to make that kind of judgement. He certainly hasn't changed the course of popular music the way they did.

ELEANOR WILLIAMS, promotions director of KJLH radio station in Los Angeles.
I think his ['Bad'] video is offensive to all black people. It contained all the stereotypical negative images of blacks - the drug dealing, the graffiti writing. He's too weird with those Elephant Man bones. Where are his values?

MUSICIANS

LEON NDUGU CHANCLER, studio drummer.
It was everybody's goal to sell ten million records again after ['Off The Wall']. Everybody came in to give it up.

I was placed in a room by myself so there was no leakage [of sound]. Both Michael and Quincy came in to suggest things for the two or three hours it took to cut the track ['Billie Jean']. I played it through about eight or ten times.

Michael and Quincy is a perfect marriage. Those guys are so in tune with each other that it makes it easy.

LOUIS JOHNSON, of Brothers Johnson, bassist.
Michael was very specific about how he wanted the bass line [to 'Billie Jean'] to go. He had me bring all my guitars to see how they sounded playing the part. I tried three or four basses before we settled on the Yamaha. It's really live with a lot of power and guts... On the basic riff I overdubbed the parts to strengthen its power.

EDDIE VAN HALEN, rock guitarist on 'Beat It'.

I did it as a favour. I didn't want nothing. Maybe Michael will give me dance lessons someday. I was a complete fool, according to the rest of the band, and our manager and everybody else. I was not used. I knew what I was doing. I don't do anything unless I want to do it.

SLASH, Guns n'Roses guitarist on 'Black Or White'.

Michael just wanted whatever was in my style. He just wanted me to do that. No pressure. He was really in sync with me. I don't come from this heavy metal school of guitar playing. All the stuff that I do or dig is from the same place that Michael Jackson comes from. We may go in separate directions or be different side of the fence but when it comes down to it, it all comes from the same shit.

JENNIFER BATTEN, band member, Dangerous tour.

Michael wanted me to dye my hair this [white] colour so I would stand out on stage. I don't mind. If that's what he wants, then that is what Michael gets.

SETH RIGGS, vocal coach.

He started out with a high voice and I've taken it even higher. He can sing low - down to a basso low C - but he prefers to sing as high as he does because pop tenors have more range to create style.

FRED ASTAIRE.

He is a wonderful mover. He makes these moves up himself and it is just great to watch. I think he just feels that way when he is singing those songs. I don't know how much more dancing he will take up, because singing and dancing at the same time is very difficult.

But Michael is a dedicated artist. He dreams, he thinks of it all the time. You can see what the result is.

GENE KELLY.

There are a lot of dancers who can go 90 miles an hour, but Michael is too clever for that.

TWYLA THARP, dancer, choreographer, dance company founder.

He's very precise. He's obviously very quick. That's been in black dancing for a long time - with the early tap dancers and the street dancers. It's part of a tradition that Michael Jackson clearly had access to. There's probably no-one so accurate and just basically sexy.

BOB FOSSE, choreographer/ producer/director.

I think he's terrific. Clean, neat, fast with a sensuality that comes through. Maybe he's more a synthesizer than innovator but it's never the steps that are most important. It's the style. That's what Michael has.

VINCE PATERSON, choreographer and video director.

Sure he's a little afraid of people. When you have people that, from the time you're a little kid, want you, they want pieces of you, they want your clothes, they want your hair - you're going to get nervous around people.

HILTON BATTLE, dancer.

It's the combinations that really distinguish him as an artist. Spin, stop, pull up leg, pull jacket open, turn, freeze. And the glide where he steps forward while pushing back. Spinning three times and popping up on his toes. That's a trademark and a move a lot of professionals wouldn't try. If you go up wrong, you can really hurt yourself.

MICHAEL WHELAN, designer working on four versions of cover to 'Victory' album.

He told me to make him pretty and paler. And after each meeting with Jackson, I had lawyers on the phone telling me to get it right.

MARK RYDEN, illustrator for 'Dangerous' album sleeve.

Michael asked for some very specific image, and on my own I made analogies to all these things I know about Michael to create images that are supposed to draw the people in. Michael wanted it to be mysterious, for people to interpret for themselves.

DENNIS TOMPKINS, designer for Bad tour.

The more an outfit weighs, the happier Michael feels.

Michael's a born stylist and I make my designs according to his suggestions. At the fittings, if he likes an item, he'll start dancing as if he were on stage. If he stays quiet, it means he doesn't like it.

He's like a kid with a new toy. Whenever he has a new costume he immediately prefers it to the ones he already has.

MICHAEL BUSH, costume designer for Dangerous tour.

Michael wanted a different look for even the most basic outfits so we went with a lot of black and gold - 18 carat of course.

Working with Michael is a unique experience. He describes what he envisions and he's so visually creative, our main goal is to bring his ideas to life. Everything you'll see on stage - every special effect - is inspired by him. We're definitely pioneering new ground with these outfits.

JOY HARRIS, literary agent.

It will be primarily pictures and drawings and poetry, and then a substantial text. You know, he's not 40-years-old, so I don't think he feels that it's time to do his autobiography, but it is time to make his statement.

DAN FRANKLIN, Heinemann editorial director.

I bought [*Moonwalk*, Jackson's autobiography] sight unseen. I paid a lot of money for it - six figures in fact. We're very excited. It's a very extraordinary man and may be a work of great literary style.

KENNY ROGERS, MICHAEL, DIANA ROSS, BARRY MANILOW AND QUINCY JONES.

VICTORY TOUR.

FRANK DILEO.

MANAGEMENT & BUSINESS DEALS

RON WEISNER, part of Weisner-DeMann management team.
They aren't exactly ready to retire at the moment. **[On The Jacksons' 10th anniversary.]**

You are dealing with family. Anything that involves a family member such as [Jermaine leaving the group] is a touchy situation. Everybody made their own personal choices, trying not to intermingle their personal lives with the business aspects.

It's a constant situation of proving yourself to the industry and to other people that you can write, you can produce, and it goes beyond a certain standpoint. Yes, you cannot complain about the success you've had in the past where you've had other people write and produce your product. But I guess everyone matures to an age where they can in turn do the same.

The tuxedo was the overall game plan for the 'Off The Wall' album and package. Michael had an image before as a young kid and all of a sudden, here was a hot album and somebody very clean-looking. The [white] socks were Michael's idea; the tuxedo was ours.

There's no great love between us [Joe Jackson and Weisner/DeMann] and it's no big secret. I haven't talked to the man in six months. But we have no problem with Michael or the Jacksons. The problem seems to be with their father... Joe doesn't talk to anybody [at Epic Records]. He doesn't have any relationship, and from what I can gather, he doesn't want to.

It was a co-management situation because Joe represented the group. But everything creative - material, marketing, promotion, whatever - was handled through this office.

FREDDIE DEMANN, part of Weisner/DeMann management team.
To use Michael's own words, "You got to put the jelly on the jelly". The jelly means the absolute best. And Michael knew he had so much jelly. **[On 'Thriller'.]**

The album ['Destiny'] is an important one musically. They've grown immensely as songwriters. The up-tempo numbers have funk, are gritty, but at the same time are happy, good-time music.

We've worked directly with the group - with Michael and the Jacksons. [Joe] hasn't been involved in any of the major issues for the past five years. We don't have a good relationship with him but I don't think he enjoys a good relationship with anyone whose skin is not black.

FRANK DILEO, former manager.
We knew that 'Billie Jean' would come on the charts at about fifty. The day we started working on [promoting] that single, we started working 'Beat It' at AOR [adult oriented rock radio]. And it built well enough at AOR that when 'Billie Jean' hit the Top Ten, we were ready to release 'Beat It' as a single - and get two singles in the Top Ten at one time. **[In fact, both singles were in the Top Five at the same time.]**

'Thriller' is not a video. We make short films that may be used for MTV or cable.

One of the things we found is that Michael's been grossly misquoted. More questions were asked about his personal life than the business end. We both feel that a person's personal life should be... personal.

Michael's only had two operations. One on his nose and one to put a cleft in his chin. All the other stuff is complete nonsense. Everybody in the world strives to look better. There's not a person in Hollywood hasn't had a nose job.

10

FRANK DILEO AND QUINCY JONES.

He loves children. You know, they're more fun to be around; adults are always on your case about something. Children are just interested in Michael as a person.

What happens if 'Bad' doesn't match 'Thriller' but ends up selling 25 million and becomes the second largest album of all time? What are people going to say? That we're losers?

Michael is a rare spirit whose special talent and achievements have lifted the standards of the recording industry and brought happiness to millions worldwide.

A trick which just doubles him up is to lure me on to the hotel balcony when he's waving at fans. Then he'll reach into my pockets, steal my cash - the $2,000 I usually carry around with me - and throw it to the crowd.

My appetite drives Michael to distraction. He thinks I'm eating my way to a heart attack and I guess he could be right... I've put on twenty pounds since we started the European leg of the ['Bad'] tour and that was only three months ago. I blame the scones.

Michael does not want to do concerts again, of any size. This will be our last tour. We wanted to make it the best and the biggest and we did it. **[End of the Bad tour.]**

It was a complete shock, a nasty surprise. Michael called out of the blue and said I was fired. Then he hung up.

JOHN BRANCA, former attorney and business adviser.

Michael is very intelligent, very smart. This is not a Colonel Tom Parker and Elvis situation. Part of him may be a ten-year-old with all the enthusiasms that implies - that's the part that gets all the publicity. But the other part is a 60-year-old genius. He's the shrewdest artist I've ever come across.

There was only one Elvis, there is only one Sinatra, there was only one Beatles, and there's only one Michael Jackson.

He wants to know about tax laws, and the difference between gross participation and the net profit definition. He loves to learn.

Michael is very informed and aware of what is going on in his life to an amazing degree. He's his own Rasputin.

I worry all the time. The Pepsi accident has caused everybody to be a little concerned... with a tour ['Victory'] of this magnitude, it's got to be planned with perfectionism to make sure it's conducted smoothly.

You couple a major blockbusting film with a major blockbusting soundtrack album. Think of the merchandising. For Michael Jackson now, the sky is the limit. **[On Michael's movie plans.]**

WALTER YETNIKOFF, former president of CBS Records.

Michael is the epitome of where popular culture is today in the US and, maybe, all over the world. He represents youth and joy and... even goodness.

I don't think the ['*Thriller*'] album's sales are finished. There are some 200 million people [in the USA] and we've sold only 18 million copies here so far. There are a few more to go.

Michael is an innovator, a pioneer. Just look at what he's done with video and music so far. He has set the standard for everyone else to follow and I believe he will be a pioneer in other things too. He loves to do things that are wildly original. In that sense, his talent is only beginning to scratch the surface.

DON DEMPSEY, Epic senior vice-president when 'Thriller' was released.

A record company is required to perform on a monthly basis. When you have a record like 'Thriller', which in one month is capable of generating $10 million to $12 million in sales, it takes pressure off the label and allows it to develop new acts.

THE VICTORY TOUR

Forget anything that has ever happened in entertainment before. This tour is Guatemala, it's El Salvador. **[Victory tour PR.]**

JOHN BRANCA.

Don King was not Michael's first choice to promote the [Victory] tour. The tour is important to Michael because it's important to Michael's family. I'm not sure the tour was Michael's first choice. He might have preferred to do other things. But he found it important to tour at his brothers' request and his family's request. They very much wanted to work with Don King.

DON KING, co-promoter of the tour.

If the boys decide to exploit every avenue of merchandising and marketing available to them - T shirts, pay-per-view TV concerts, clothing lines, perfume lines, product identification - the tour could gross $100 million.

DON KING WITH THE JACKSONS BEFORE THE VICTORY TOUR.

With Michael, you are always on trial.

Michael's doing the tour to help his family. I feel this will be the last tour that Michael will do with them.

CHUCK SULLIVAN, tour promoter who suffered a heart attack during Victory tour and lost money after it.
There are disparate personalities with a diversity of interests, it's a difficult thing. People who are closely associated with Michael - Branca, Dileo - just want to get the thing over with. And people who are associated with the brothers look at it as the most significant career opportunity they will have. They want to maximise the return on that. I think Don King's interest has been in establishing a beach head in the music promotion business.

LARRY LARSON, Victory tour co-ordinator.
If I can hang in there and ride the bucking bronco, then at the end of the tour, if the Jacksons end up earning millions and millions of dollars, I'm looking good. That's going to give me a credit to go for a Rolling Stones tour. I'd love to do a Rolling Stones tour.

REV AL SHARPTON, after The Jacksons had been pressurised into playing 'black' cities, co-promoting with local promoters.
I feel the Jackson family has set a pace and a pattern that should be followed by all black superstars. I am very happy that The Jacksons have agreed to go into those major markets and use those minority promoters they've always used... hopefully The Jacksons' decision will be a beacon light to other entertainers that you don't forget where you come from.

THE PEPSI DEALS

ROGER ENRICO, Pepsi chief executive officer, on the 1986 advertising deal.
It's more than $5m and less than $15m.

Our business saw a major upswing and it has been on a roll ever since. **[Thirty days after screening the 1984 ads.]**

This new relationship will be the most comprehensive, the most significant, the most far-reaching ever between a corporation and a performing artist.

JAY COLEMAN of Rockbill, the company which got the two parties together.
The key to making the connection between The Jacksons and Pepsi was that few groups in popular music have the broad audience identification of Michael and his brothers. The Jacksons have the young people and also can attract their mothers, who control the purchases at home.

Eyewitness at the accident during filming of a Pepsi advertisement.
Two canisters went off and Michael's head caught fire. Everyone was screaming at him but he didn't take any notice. Then he put up the collar of his jacket and suddenly fell to the floor with flames shooting several feet in the air from his head. He was in agony and people rushed to help him.

He was wonderful. He reassured people even as he was being taken away on a stretcher.

THE LA GEAR DEAL

RANDY PHILLIPS, intermediary in LA Gear endorsement deal.
John [Branca] said that Michael was thinking of wearing sneakers instead of his black loafers

when he made his new videos for his upcoming greatest hits album. It was obvious that the switch to sneakers was a pretty radical image change.

The LA Gear guys were desperate to get involved, no matter what the cost, with someone of Michael's stature... He was the opposite of what I expected - he was very warm and conversational, and asked very sharp questions about marketing and promotion.

Michael may have said only two sentences, but he spoke more at our Press conference than he did at Pepsi's... or when he visited the White House for that matter... He came to the Press conference wearing LA Gear's hottest shoes. You didn't see him ever drinking a Pepsi at their Press conference.

NIKE

LEONARD MARKS, Apple Corporation lawyer suing Nike who had acquired 'Revolution' from Michael Jackson, owner of The Beatles' song catalogue.
The Beatles want to stop advertisers from jumping on the bandwagon by trying to sell their products by association with The Beatles and their music.

JON PETERS, co-chairman of Columbia Pictures Entertainment.
I said to Michael, "Close your eyes. Picture yourself getting out of a limo. You open your eyes and it's an art deco building that says Michael Jackson Entertainment Company on top. You walk in the lobby and there are guys with epaulettes and hats standing there. It's your family, your home, and you're the boss."

MICHAL SCHULHOF, vice-chairman Sony USA.
If Michael continues to perform the way he has

in the past, both he and we will do very well. He's a 33-year-old. I don't think anybody, including Michael himself, can predict how he is going to exercise that creativity. It may be in music, it may be in film, it may be in totally new areas of entertainment. The fact that the [$65m] contract with him is unique reflects the fact that he is a unique talent.

BOB JONES, Michael Jackson Productions.
Since I've been here, Michael has been in complete control. He knows what works for him and for the public. He's much more fixed in his ideas as to how he wants to do things.

GOLLY GALLAGHER, record promoter who invited Jackson to his birthday party at JW's nightclub in Camberley. Jackson was in France at the time.
I invited him because he's an old friend but until he walked through the door I had no idea whether he would turn up. He's a really nice guy, very quiet and is enjoying himself upstairs and will probably stay until he's bored.

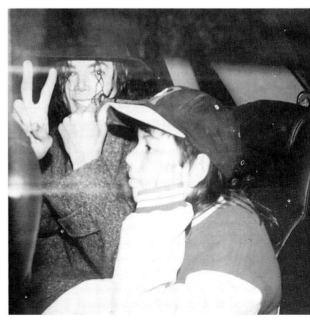

MICHAEL WITH BROOKE SHIELDS AND EMMANUEL LEWIS, STAR OF THE TV SHOW WEBSTER IN 1984.

CELEBRITIES

DIANA ROSS.
I'm very happy to have been able to give a nationally well-deserving group an opportunity to perform because that's how we, The Supremes, got our big chance. Had it not been for Berry Gordy searching for talent in our black community, we wouldn't have been discovered. **[Introducing, though not discovering, the Jackson 5.]**

There was an identification between Michael and I. I was older, he kind of idolised me, and he wanted to sing like me.

Michael has a lot of people around him but he's very afraid. I don't know why. I think it came from the early days.

I care for Michael but I don't worry about him. I think sometimes that he's got angels on his shoulders to protect him.

He spends a lot of time - too much - by himself. I try to get him out. I rented a boat and took my children and Michael on a cruise and he loved it. He has so many people around him but he's still afraid, especially to be alone at night. I don't know why but he's always been very cut off and distanced. When you get to be a star from age six and never knew any normal teenage life, when you were just used to the limousines and the tour buses, I guess it is understandable.

I know him so well but sometimes I'm even stunned at how he can be so shy. He'll hide and talk in a whisper then you let him on stage and he turns into this sexy, macho thing. I try to get him to step out socially, to get a little more out of himself because he spends a lot of time, too much time, by himself. **[After he'd co-written and produced 1985's 'Eaten Alive!', her LP title track.]**

He really did want to be me almost down, right down to gestures and vocal tricks, even clothes. **[At one time or another it has been alleged that Michael's facial surgery has** been devised so that he might look like Ross, his sister LaToya, his sister Janet or that he simply did not want to look like his father, Joe.]**

I wish Berry Gordy were here tonight to be part of this. I'm sure he remembers Michael's Emmy-nominated performance on the Motown 25 special. **[Commenting as Michael wins seven categories plus special Award Of Merit at American Music Awards.]**

JANE FONDA.
Dad was also painfully self-conscious and shy in life and he really only felt comfortable behind the mask of a character. He could liberate himself when he was someone else. That's a lot like Michael. In some ways, Michael reminds me of the walking wounded. He's an extremely fragile person. I think that just getting on with life, making contact with people is hard enough, much less to be worried about whither goest the world.

Michael's got a fresh, original sound. The music is energetic, and it's sensual. You can dance to it, work out to it, make love to it, sing to it. It's hard to sit still to.

On some level, I don't even know whether it's conscious or not, Michael has to stand off the demands of reality and protect himself.

His intelligence is instinctual and emotional, like a child's. If any artist loses that childlikeness, you lose a lot of creative juice. So Michael creates around himself a world that protects his creativity.

He's a miracle. He has so much talent; the more he gives, the more he seems to have. I'm proud to be his friend.

PAUL McCARTNEY.
I didn't get destroyed by [press and fanmania] and neither will Michael. He's very talented. He knows how to make records that people like. But he's a very straightforward kid. He has a great deal of faith. He's got a lot of innocence - he protects that especially. Michael looks at cartoons all day and keeps away from drugs. That's how he maintains his innocence.

Most of us fellas at 13 or 14 are trying to make our voices break so the girls will go out with us. But someone who is making so much money out of not being butch, as Michael is, wouldn't want his voice to break. He just doesn't want to lose his childhood, I know the feeling. 'Thriller' sells here not because he's some kind of jerk. It's proof that he's reaching the people. To hell with the snobs who think fame is rathah vulgah, dahling.

He has a great voice, a freshness and energy that is infectious, and he's a fabulous dancer.

It's [like] getting an audience with the Pope. He broke eight lunch appointments in a row. **[On trying to meet Michael.]**

LIONEL RICHIE.
I wouldn't have minded stroking the deer and all but I was really hungry at the time. Michael didn't have any conception of time. I asked him did he wear a watch and he just shrugged "Nu huh. What is time, anyway?"

SMOKEY ROBINSON.
Predicting the future for Michael Jackson is very difficult, because he's already broken all artistic barriers... I know that there's even more to come for him, more peaks and successes.

STEVIE WONDER.
Michael's a natural... he's a very hard worker and a super performer. But most of all, he's a real human being.

It has taken some people quite a few years and millions of pop hit records to realise what I knew and felt from the very beginning. The Jacksons have been and continue to be the most talented family in the history of show business.

BOY GEORGE [on telephoning Michael].
It takes him half an hour to say one word. It's almost like you want to put something in his tea to get him going.

THOMAS DOLBY.
[Michael] said come over so I staggered up the drive in the pouring rain, lit by headlights from one of the limos, and rang the doorbell. And there was a kind of Busby Berkeley staircase in there, and he came down wearing what appeared to be pink pyjamas. He climbed into this throne, a big medieval chair, and we got to talking about music and the weather and he was very sweet, actually.

We got on very well, we've got a lot in common though I'm nowhere near as eccentric as him.

STEVIE WONDER, QUINCY JONES, DIONNE WARWICK, MICHAEL, AND LIONEL RICHIE.

I thought we were alone in the house but then I noticed little faces kept peering through the banisters. And a door burst open and 'She Blinded Me With Science' [Dolby's hit] came blasting out of another room and the faces reappeared and they were giggling. I said "What's with them?" Michael said, "Oh, they're just my cousin's schoolfriends. They come over on a Thursday and play here". I said, "What do they find so funny?" And he said, "Oh, they just can't believe you're the guy off the TV".

HENRY MANCINI.
Take a fellow as mercurial as Michael Jackson. Quincy was the levelling agent for him. He was the producer who brought it out of Michael.

MICHAEL LOVESMITH.
Don't believe all this nonsense about Michael being gay and stuff. When there were girls around he'd talk about them to the guys and run around pinching their asses and then run away. He was a real funky street dude, know what I mean?

JIMMY OSMOND [formerly Little Jimmy of The Osmonds].
People in Japan tend to look inside a person and they see that "so what if he appears a little weird, he's a cool guy inside".

PRINCE [by an observer at their meeting].
They kind of sat there, checking each other out but said very little. It was a fascinating stalemate between two very powerful dudes.

NELSON GEORGE.
Michael is not an experimenter like Prince, it takes him a long time to get what he wants. He's a perfectionist. He was very scared of finishing [the album 'Bad']. The closer he got to completing it the more terrified he became of the confrontation with the public. He's more Cab Calloway than Duke Ellington. He's very comfortable with that whole white Broadway *Sound Of Music* type thing, the musical heritage. He's kind of Bing Crosby.

GLADYS KNIGHT.

We go back a really long ways. I'm talking about our theatre days when The Jacksons used to come up to the Regal Theater in Chicago. I remember Michael's legs weren't long enough to reach the floor when he was sitting down. That was '65 or '66.

Joe used to come around and talk to me and [our manager] Taylor Cox. One night they had a talent show at the [Regal] Theater and I told Joe we were going to get somebody out there to see them. So they went on and everybody loved them and the next thing I know - big headlines - Diana Ross discovers the Jackson 5! Hey, great, that's all well and good, as long as they were discovered, you know what I mean?

As far as I'm concerned Michael still sings as beautiful as ever. He will learn as he gets older that the older you get, the more appreciated your talent is in the industry.

ELIZABETH TAYLOR.

He is so giving of himself that, at times, he leaves very little to protect that beautiful inner core that is the essence of him.

LIZA MINELLI.

He's a wonderful friend to have.

MADONNA.

I have this whole vision about Michael. We're considering working on a song together. I would like to completely re-do his whole image - give him a Caesar - you know, that really short haircut - and I want to get him out of those buckly boots and all that stuff. What I want him to do is go to New York and hang out for a week with the House Of Extravaganza [a group of voguers]... give him a new style.

He's up for a couple of things that surprise me. The thing is, I'm not going to get together and do some stupid ballad or love duet - no-one's going to buy it. I said "Look, Michael, if you want to do something with me, you have to be willing to go all the way or I'm not going to do it." He keeps saying yes.

SHIRLEY MURDOCK (who recorded 'Superstar', a riposte to 'Billie Jean').

Michael was being provocative and ungentlemanly. His record made good business sense but mine came from the heart. For every man hurt by the Billie Jean syndrome there are twelve girls left holding the baby.

YVONNE GAGE (who recorded 'Doin' It In A Haunted House', after 'Thriller').

I hope [Michael] won't be offended. I'm his number one fan and would love to meet him. A lot of people have interpreted the song as being about sex but I prefer to think about it as togetherness. I don't think it's vulgar. I think it's rather discreet.

YVONNE FAIR (Jackson 5's opening act in 1971.)

They captivate you because Michael works the stage like an old professional. His riffs take an average singer a lifetime to learn. It's a group that lacks nothing.

LENA HORNE.

Michael is an enormous talent; I respect and adore him. When people ask me who's going to replace me in show business, I say "Michael's going to replace everyone".

BO DEREK (after a visit).

You have to sign releases that you won't tell anybody what happened.

MICHAEL WITH MADONNA.

1993 UPDATE

In February of 1993 Michael broke his 10 year silence to give a 70 minute interview with US media star Oprah Winfrey. Watched by over 60 million people throughout the world, it was a wide ranging discussion which covered all the controversial issues which have dogged Michael over the past decade, and his purpose in granting the interview in the first place seems to have been to lay waste the rumours which have inspired such nicknames as 'Wacko Jacko'.

The interviews took place in Southern California at Michael's 27,000 acre Neverland Valley Ranch in Santa Ynez where he maintains a private fairground and zoo, and where his house guests are almost always handicapped children who can take best advantage of the facilities.

Dressed in the now traditional black pants and red buttoned-up shirt with military style collar and epaulettes and a rather sinister black armband, Michael began by looking back over his long career, showing footage of the Jackson 5 rehearsing and auditioning before Berry Gordy, the founder of Motown Records. Even then it was obvious that Michael was the star of the show.

"James Brown was a genius," he told Oprah after a sequence in which a tiny Michael pirouetted in a manner undoubtedly inspired by the Godfather of Soul. "I used to watch him on TV. Also Jackie Wilson... what a great entertainer he was."

He denied that his brothers were jealous of his superior talents and abilities, either then or now. "I love my family very much and I would like to see them more often," he said, before denying that he had read the controversial book by sister Latoya, now the black sheep of the Jackson clan. "I always see her as the happy Latoya I grew up with."

But happiness, it appeared, was not an abundant commodity in the Jackson household.
"The stage was my home," Michael told Oprah. "Once I got off stage I was very sad... sad at having to face the popularity and all that. There were times when I had a great time with my brothers, pillow fights and things, but I'd always cry from loneliness."

Michael admitted that his childhood had been blighted by a lack of contact with any children other than his brothers. He described how he would walk home from school and pass other kids playing in parks. He was unable to join them because he was always due home for a rehearsal. "You don't get to do the things that other children do," he said. "I compensate for that now by having children around because when I was little it was always work, work, work."

Adolescence, it seems, was little better. "Every child star suffers through this period because you're not the cute and charming child that you were, and you start to grow and they - the public - want to keep you young forever and little

12

MICHAEL IN DISGUISE IN LOS ANGELES.

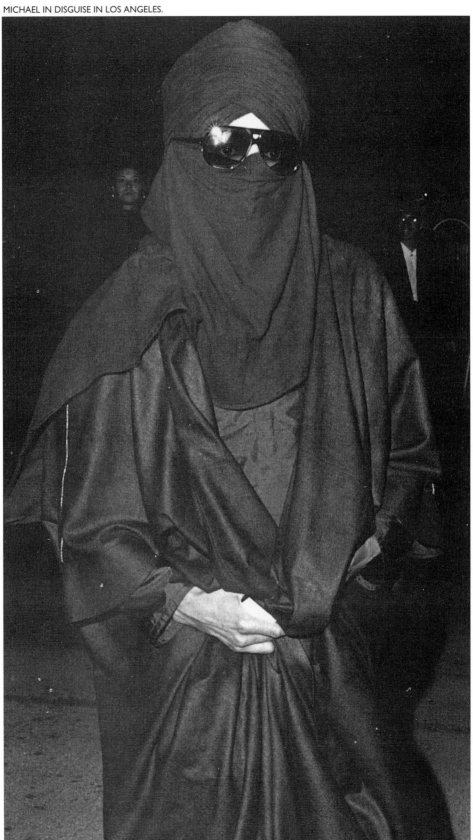

forever." Neither was Michael spared from the normal problems faced by teenagers. "I had pimples so bad, it made me so shy. I used to not look at myself, I'd wash my face in the dark. I wouldn't want to look in the mirror and my father teased me and I hated it, and I cried every day because of it. He would tell me I was ugly."

Michael's relationship with his father was evidently a stormy affair. "I love my father but I don't know him," he said. "My mother's wonderful. To me she's perfection... I just wish I could understand my father." Michael confirmed the stories in Latoya's book that his father beat him. "He saw me as his golden child or whatever. Some might call him a strict disciplinarian or whatever but he's strict, very hard, very stern... just a look would scare you. I was very frightened of him. There were times when he'd come to see me and I would get sick. I'd start to regurgitate... both as a child and an adult."

Michael said he had forgiven his father, just as he had by now forgiven the newspapers and magazines which printed unflattering - and untrue - stories about him. "There's so much garbage written about me," he said with a trace of anger - even bewilderment - in his voice. "It's so untrue and they're complete lies. These are some of the things that I want to talk about," he said, warming to the theme of what was obviously his real reason for giving the interview in the first place.

"The press have made up some Godawful horrifying stories that are completely appalling, so far from the truth," he continued. "It has made me realise that the more times you hear a lie, you begin to believe it. It's appalling the things that have been said about me and they're completely false."

The first rumour that Michael dealt with was that he slept in an oxygen tank. "I did a commercial for Pepsi and I was burned very badly. We settled for

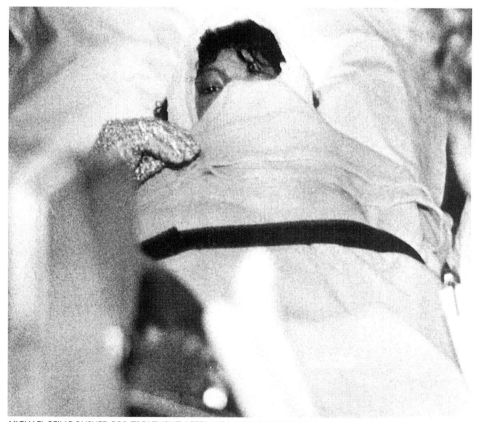

MICHAEL BEING RUSHED FOR TREATMENT AFTER HIS HAIR CAUGHT FIRE DURING THE FILMING OF A PEPSI COLA COMMERCIAL IN 1984.

one million dollars and with the money we built this Michael Jackson Burns Centre." Michael explained that among the facilities in the centre was a bed-like plastic covered device similar to a large incubator in which a burns victim would lie for treatment, and Michael himself went inside the device, lying down flat to check it out. "Someone takes a picture and when they process the picture someone says, 'Oh Michael Jackson'. He makes a copy and sends it all over the world with this lie attached to it... why do

people buy these papers and it's not the truth. I'm here to say, 'Do not judge a person'."

Michael also denied the story that he had bought the bones of the Elephant Man, the name given to the horribly deformed John Merrick who lived in London at the turn of the century and whose case became a *cause célèbre* . Finally, Michael dealt with the rumour that he had somehow bleached his skin in order to become more white. "There is no such thing as skin bleaching," he said before admitting that he had a skin disorder which destroyed the pigmentation and which had become apparent around the time he recorded 'Off The Wall' and 'Thriller'. "It is something which I cannot help," he said. "It is in my family on my father's side. I use make-up to even out the blotches. When people make up stories that I don't want to be who I am it hurts me."

On the verge of crying Michael declared firmly that he was proud to be a black American, and was certainly not ashamed of the colour of his skin. He drew a parallel with sunbathing. "What about all the millions of people who sit out in the sun to become darker, to become other than what they are. No one says anything about that." He did concede that he'd had some plastic surgery on his nose, but denied that any surgery had been performed on his cheekbones, eyes or lips.

Turning to his personal life - and sex - Michael confirmed he was dating Brooke Shields, but that they met mostly at their respective homes rather than go out where they would be recognised. "Yes, I've been in love," he said, rather coyly. "With Brooke and with someone else." In the now famous exchange following Oprah's inquiry about whether he was a virgin, Michael replied: "I'm a gentleman. That is something that's private. Call me old fashioned... I'm embarrassed." As to whether he would eventually marry and raise a family of his own, Michael said he wasn't yet ready because he was married to his work. "I admire children, but I am married to my music."

It was unquestionably the frankest interview Michael had given in years though some commentators later suggested it was stage managed to promote the acceptable image that Michael seeks. He hadn't spoken to journalists before, he said, because he hadn't anything to say at any time in the last ten years. But with his silence broken, are his fans any wiser about what motivates Michael than they were before?